Bleak Walls, Bright Minds

Why this book? Why now? The simple answer to those questions is *because it is time* for people to hear incarcerated men and women **In Their Own Words**.

I am a retired family and substance abuse therapist. I began working with inmates, referred to as clients in my profession, and their loved ones 20 years ago.   My husband and I worked together under contract with the Federal Bureau of Prisons in Las Cruces NM, assisting clients during early re-entry after lengthy periods of incarceration. The government program was called TDAT, Transitional Drug and Alcohol Treatment. As a therapist, I saw clients twice weekly, once individually and once for group. The client had the option of family counseling with me also and many took advantage of that opportunity. When I retired 10 years ago, and returned to Iowa, I got involved in several non-profit organizations to continue my involvement with the incarcerated and their loved ones and to become active in prison reform. I founded Living Beyond the Bars of Iowa (LBTB's) to support the loved ones of those incarcerated persons. I believe in prison reform and reconciliation.

Because of my focus on working with and emotionally supporting loved ones of the incarcerated, I became involved with the effort to pass the lifer relief bill, HF2533, 18 months ago. I continue to work toward lifer relief through all the organizations I am part of and am privileged to be on the team drafting the current bill to be presented in 2021. As a team, we agree lifer's deserve consideration for a second chance.

As a family therapist I was extremely interested in brain maturity and since retirement I continue to stay current on developments in that area of human growth. We now understand the human brain does not mature until a human's early to mid-twenties. I, along with numerous other professionals and lay people, believe this fact is **crucial** and a **compelling factor** that needs to be considered in determining sentencing for crimes, especially in the area of Life With Out Parole.

Due to all the roles I play today, I have been fortunate to have conversations with numerous people doing Life With Out Parole (LWOP) in Iowa, through phone conversations, o-mail accounts (email for offenders) and/or written letters. I have sat with numerous of their loved ones and learned how they keep relationships with family alive. I have seen and heard how the lifers help other inmates as mentors and by providing Hospice care. And I have seen the contributions they have made through giving of their time and money to people in need in society. But most importantly, I have witnessed how many lifers have developed into responsible, reformed, and mature adults with strong values of compassion, honesty and being examples of how one can turn his/her life around. My hope is you will gain an eye into these people through these pages and may even decide to become active in reform yourself.

So, Why This? Why Now? It's the best way I can think of to share what I have seen and learned with you, **In Their Own Words**.

Sue Hutchins, founder of Living Beyond the Bars of Iowa

"A bend in the road is not the end of the road...Unless you fail to make the turn."
— Helen Keller

All of us are better than the worst thing we have ever done and worse than the best thing we have ever done

A few other things you should know

We, The Lifer Review Team, introduced a bi-partician Iowa Second Chance Lifer Bill in February 2020. HF2433. It made it into the Public Safety sub-committee and received a lot of support from numerous groups and individuals, including legislators. Our team has used that bill as the foundation for a bill that will be introduced in the 2021 Iowa legislature. It again has bi-partician support.

We are aware there are a number of other states also considering this kind of legislation, and acknowledge a special thank you to The Sentencing Project out of Washington DC for providing a regular zoom meeting for all of us to support one another and share our perceptions to effect change.

3

We are also aware there is an appetite to raise the age of adulthood from 18 to 25 with regards to sentencing a person as a juvenile or as an adult. This is based on well accepted scientific evidence of how and when the human brain develops and achieves maturity. We are in support of making changes in the laws because of this evidence and hopeful we will see changes soon based on this knowledge.

Here are this bill's Talking Points:

Lifer Review Legislation

The safety valve of commutation is broken for Iowans serving life sentences, leaving inmates without hope or justice, keeping prisons overcrowded and inefficient, and creating a major tax burden on the public. The Iowa constitution grants the governor the power to commute prison sentences and release individuals—even lifers—when appropriate. Historically, Iowa governors have used this power as a safety valve to ensure justice for rehabilitated inmates, maintain safety inside our prisons, and ensure that the state budget is used responsibly. Between 1945 and 1982, 195 commutations were granted for exactly this purpose. Since 1983, however, only 10 commutations have been granted. **The system has become stacked against commutation.** Lifers are allowed to apply only once every ten years. Applications go to the parole board which has bureaucratic rules that contain no time limitations and require a unanimous vote for a recommendation for commutation. Since 2009, only 3 out of 84 applications received that unanimous favorable vote. **With our prisons 6% overcrowded and a recession underway, it is critical that we fix the safety valve of commutation.**

This new legislation would create a more robust review process to ensure a meaningful second look at certain life sentences.

- After serving 25 years of their sentence, lifers in minimum custody status would be allowed to apply for commutation every three years.
- A Life Imprisonment Review Committee, a dedicated group of unpaid volunteers, would be created to conduct intensive reviews of applications for commutation and then make recommendations to the governor and parole board.
- The governor retains the constitutional power to grant or deny commutation, but this legislation provides her/him with stronger grounds and more detailed recommendations to make these critical decisions. It also gives her/him an alternative in which s/he can allow a case to return to the district court for limited review and reconsideration by the judge.
- Recommendations and district court decisions would be based on a set of factors aimed at identifying rehabilitation and justice considerations in the case.

Inmates will have real hope for full rehabilitation.

- Research has shown that carefully vetted applicants for commutation paroled later in life are extremely unlikely to commit subsequent violent crimes. In Iowa, the recidivism rate for released lifers for whom data is available is **-0-**.
- Improving access to commutation reunites families

Iowa's prisons will be safer and less crowded.

- By focusing narrowly on the strongest candidates for commutation, this legislation is a crucial first step in "right-sizing" our prisons, reducing overcrowding, and ending over-incarceration in Iowa.
- As lifers work toward the real possibility of commutation and release, they will

The public will have their tax dollars used more efficiently.

- The current, broken commutation process keeps many people incarcerated even after they have "aged out" of crime.
- Currently, tax-payers foot the bill for the high cost of providing medical care and suitable housing for these older inmates.
- Commutation of these older

and allows these individuals to make positive contributions to their communities

make conditions better for everyone incarcerated with them.

inmates keeps the cost of our prisons lower and saves tax-payer dollars.

Tim Diesburg

I worked for the IDOC for almost 36 years, and I currently serve as Vice Chair on the IDOC IPI since I retired December 2018. I've known and worked with hundreds of lifers in my career with the Iowa Department of Corrections (IDOC), and I'll be the first to tell you, most are where they should be. I can also tell you, I know there are some who have served many years 20- 25- and 30 plus years, and I believe they have served their debt to society, and if released they would do very well as a returned citizen. In fact, they would be so grateful for the chance to prove themselves, they would be positive successful people. I have watch many of these lifers grow from immature young people in their teens and twenties, grow into middle aged adults. Many of them have come to appreciate the magnitude of harm they caused to others and feel very ashamed of what they did in their younger years. They deeply regret their actions and try to give back as much as they can when given the chance. I've seen them gain meaningful education such as college degrees, including getting their master's degree, gain their education and technical skills through registered apprenticeship occupations and on the job training. We need to give these lifers something to work toward and give them a purpose and hope.

Here is a list of different Governors and the number of sentences they commuted.
The juvenile lifers would not be included in the commutation process since they were resentenced after the Supreme Court ruling. All serving life without parole.

Governor	Term	Commuted
Robert Blue	1945-49	16
William Beardsley	1949-54	26
Leo Elthon	1954-57	30
Hershel Loveless	1957-61	46
Norman Erbe	1961-63	11
Harold Hughes	1963-69	39
Robert Fulton	15 Days	00
Robert Ray	1969-83	27
Terry Branstad	1983-99	2
Tom Vilsack	1999-2007	7
Chester Culver	2007-11	0
Terry Branstad	2011- 2017	1
Kim Reynolds	2017 -	0

Juvenile Lifers Sentences Commuted 38 Juvenile Lifers due to Supreme Court Law
2020 There are 736 (44 Female, 692 Male) Lifers with no chance of parole within the IDOC

8

Lifers serving 25 years and more, 301 (16 Female, 285 Male) (with no chance of parole)
195 commuted between 1945 and 1983 and only 10 in the last 37 years.

A person (incarcerated or not) with no purpose can be very dangerous. If the lifers in Iowa had a purpose to work toward, it would make our correctional facilities much much safer to work in and offenders to live in. I understand there are many people who have never been given the chance to see these offenders in a way I have, see them mature, grow, and improve themselves over time. I've also seen them become very successful while incarcerated! Many of us long time staff, including Wardens and Treatment Directors have witnessed these transformations. I feel a great passion to help in Justice reform and a I believe one of our states shortfalls is our Life sentencing without parole and the need to change the law to 25 to life with the possibility of parole and to reform our commutation process for non – juvenile lifers. With all that said, we will still need to continue our commitment to victims and their families. I believe we can do both.

Tim Diesburg
Address: 22484 Ridge Rd E28 Anamosa Iowa, 52205
Cell Ph. 319-310-1229
Email: ahawkiam@gmail.com

Heal the Family that I Victimized

John H. Epps

In this world we live in many have been a victim of some crime, even a heinous crime. Some families have been victimized by the crime of murder. Their loved one had become a victim of a carnivorous assailants' craving. The Hebrew word for those been torn by such a crime is called "tereif." I have absorbed the impact statements of families that were victimized by murder. They expressed being torn, their insides being ripped out and their mind shredded.

They try to tell themselves their loved ones didn't die in vain. They believe in a sense that loved was some offering for the higher good. The Hebrew for offering is "Corban."

I have been in prison for nearly forty years for first degree murder. I have come to have empathy for the family I victimized and even other families. I had wondered about what I can do to amend my ways and help ease the pain that has afflicted others. I have over the years reached remorse and repented for my transgressions. I not only broke the law in humanity society, but the law of God.

Going to God about this provided healing for my mind, body and soul. This assisted me into changing for the higher good.

I have prayed for that surviving members of that family, that they be healed. I pray for other families that have been torn by participating in programs that offering talks of forgiveness. Forgiveness doesn't deny that an evil has occurred.

In spite of the evil there is a moving forward to live a life of healing. Someone asked me once, "John, "You can never give back or replace the life you have taken. Given a second chance to make amends, what would you want to do, and hope that the family would be in agreement with it: My Response:

Apologize to the family for the unimaginable tearing I have caused the. I would try to convey to them their loved one didn't deserve to be treated in such a criminal way. I would try to encourage them their loved one didn't die in vain.

True, they were an innocent victim. I want to make sure that their innocent life wasn't wasted. I owe it to the family and myself to show the change that has occurred in my life has created a new opportunity, which proves their life was not in vain.

Gary Titus

I am a lifer from Des Moines, Iowa with 32 years in prison for my role in a felony where a murder occurred, though not by my hands. As a lifer in Iowa, there is but one chance at freedom — a commutation of sentence by the Governor. The commutation process used to be very productive and very fruitful for the criminal justice system.

From 1945 to 1983 there were 211 commutations granted to inmates serving LWOP sentences in Iowa. From 1983 to 2020, there were 10 commutations granted. This was a dramatic decrease — from 211 in 38 years to 10 in 37 years. The lifer population in those 38 years prior to 1983 was SUBSTANTIALLY lower than the population we have today in Iowa. It should go without saying that a large percentage of Iowa's lifers prior to 1983 had a great deal of hope that if they do the right things and make the right changes during their incarceration, they would be given a REAL chance at life outside of prison. Clearly, not all lifers were given that chance — some due to their refusal to change and some due to the nature of their crime — but many had to believe they had a chance and naturally worked toward gaining that opportunity.

Why the dramatic decrease in commutations? Did the men and women serving MOP suddenly become less worthy of having their sentences commuted than their predecessors? Did those granted commutation do something horrendous to render the commutation system no longer a viable option? Did Iowa's citizens become outraged that those deemed worthy of a second chance by the justice system — as provided by Iowa's Constitution — were being returned to society?

The answer to ALL these questions is a resounding NO. Iowa's commutation system fell under the same arbitrary and political "get tough on crime and criminals" mentality of the 1980s and 1990s that has so harmed the criminal justice system as we know it today. In the mid-1990s the Iowa Code, section 902.2, was changed concerning commutation for lifers. Prior to this change, the Board of Parole (BOP) reviewed EVERY lifer on the fifth, tenth, thirteenth, and fifteenth year of incarceration and yearly thereafter for possible recommendation for the commutation of sentence. Today, there is no review by the BOP unless the class "A" felon applies for commutation consideration, and that application process can only happen once every ten years.

History reflects that, under the old system, the success of Iowa lifers released from prison through the commutation process, using careful screening by the BOP and the Governor, was very high. In fact, no other grouping of paroled inmates has been as successful upon release. Of the 33 former lifers released on commutation since 1970, only one returned to prison with a subsequent felony, while only four others returned on parole violations. That is a recidivism rate of only 8.25 percent!

However, the story here is bigger than the systems failings to live up to the productive system it once had been. In *Vinter and Others v. United Kingdom* - a case that outlawed life without parole sentences in the U.K. — Judge Power-Forde wrote, "Hope is an important and constitutive aspect of the human person. Those who commit the most abhorrent and egregious of acts and who inflict untold suffering upon others, nevertheless retain their fundamental humanity and carry within themselves the capacity to change. ... To deny them the experience of hope would be to deny a fundamental aspect of their humanity and, to do that, would be degrading."

I came to prison in 1988, turning 19 four days after I was sentenced to life without parole. The first 10 years of my sentence were tumultuous to say the least. I believed I was doing a life sentence for someone else's murder, and as a result, I failed to see my own culpability in my crime. While no one wants to be forever judged for the worst thing they've done, it's even harder to be forever judged for the worst thing someone else has done. But, like most other humans, I grew up. I came to a place of needing to take responsibility for my choices and actions. I did not like the person I'd become. I also realized that person would never be considered for commutation and would surely die in prison.

So I embarked on change. Not just change to impress a BOP and a Governor. I knew that would be superficial and have no real impact for good upon myself or those around me. I set out to tip the scales of my life from the overwhelming bad I'd done to at least balance it out with an equal amount of good. I needed not only to change behaviors, I had to understand why I chose to behave the way I did in the first place. I had to learn my own psychology and come up with deep rooted solutions to deep rooted problems in order to become a better person in a real, lasting, and impactful way. Yes, my upbringing was difficult. I wasn't parented well. I was also homeless at the age of 17 after being kicked out of my home. That could explain why I was in the position to make the choices I made, but it did not explain the choices themselves nor did it excuse the outcome of those choices. All of this I had to learn mostly on my own as the system offers little to no help for the lifers because they save that help for those who are getting out.

Looking back on that journey, I'd say it was a success. Maybe I've yet to fully balance the scale — I guess I have to leave that for others to decide — but I do know there is real and significant change from the teenager who committed the crime to the 51-year-old man I am today. I also know that if given the chance at freedom, with the plan laid out before me, I could definitely tip that scale all the way to the good. These changes were right for me from an overall big picture view of life, but... What does it mean for my future?

I used to believe and have spent the past 23 years believing it could mean a commutation of my sentence and a second chance at life. I have a commutation application on the Governor's desk myself and should be seeing the BOP in the coming months. But Governor Reynolds recently denied a commutation to a woman most people in the state believed she would grant. Where do the rest of the lifers in Iowa go with that decision? We had so much hope for this Governor. She talked so often about being a Governor of second chances. For the first time in my 32 years, we had a Governor coming into the prisons — even the penitentiary in Anamosa — and talking about reform and her desires to give second chances to those who've done the work to earn one. She even said in a speech at the women's prison in Mitchellville that Iowa lawmakers had a "moral responsibility to think differently" in regard to the criminal justice system. Add that to the fact that she has two drunk driving convictions of her own and knows firsthand the power of a second chance, and hope was obviously ignited within the prisons and the lifers. But then she denied a 74-year-old woman her last real shot at freedom, even though she had the lowest level of culpability in the crime committed and had the recommendation of the State Attorney General.

There is something that happens to many of Iowa's lifers I've come to refer to as the serenity of hopelessness. There is a marked measure of peace that tends to wash over someone when they truly give up hope. They don't have to strive to achieve anymore.

They don't have to worry about having a perfect prison record anymore (because it takes a near perfect record for any real consideration to be given to you). They don't have to worry about anything anymore because hey are simply waiting to die. There is, ironically and sadly, peace in that. Some like myself and that 74-year-old grandmother mentioned earlier fight against it and hold out hope that there is light at the end of the tunnel, even if the system has made the light impossible to see. Many others unfortunately succumb to it and become the walking dead. Their humanity and dignity have been stripped from them along with their hope to the point that they are just a state number in a prison cell waiting to die. I've heard it said by many that the death penalty would have been easier.

That's what our system has done to people. I fight against that serenity and continue to hold out hope, even though realistically I don't know that there truly is hope. I'm not naive to the fact that there are likely people out there who believe those with life sentences SHOULD have their humanity and dignity stripped away. There are people who believe we SHOULD have no hope. But shouldn't the first aspect of criminal justice be to correct behavior? it is called the Iowa Department of Corrections not the Iowa Department of Revenge for a reason.

I do not want to die in prison due to a broken, overly politicized criminal justice system. If I had to die in prison as a consequence of horrible actions and choices I made, that would be one thing. But Iowa's commutation history reflects that had I committed my crime a few decades earlier, that wouldn't be the case as I've done the work to change. I've maintained a good prison record for more than 20 years. I've advanced my education. I've developed vast job training skills. I've maintained and cultivated relationships within the community. I have a solid reentry plan with established housing and employment working for a ministry in Oskaloosa. I've paid my restitution in full. I've even saved a large sum of money over many years through my meager prison wages to have the resources necessary to rebuild a life out there. I just need the system to give me the chance the Iowa Constitution allows me to receive.

I've currently served 32 years of a Life Without Parole Sentence for my role in a robbery in which a man was murdered, though not by my hands. In that 32 years I have worked hard to not only change my behavior but to understand the reasons behind the behavior and work to change the thoughts and values driving those behaviors. Though not fully inclusive, below is a list of things I've done and accomplished during my incarceration to better myself, my environment, and those around me.

- Completed my high school diploma.
- Currently two courses away from earning an Associate degree from Ohio University.
- Became Literary Certified in Braille through the Library of Congress and gained ten years of experience transcribing and producing Braille for the sight-impaired students of Iowa.

- Using the pay earned while producing Braille for Iowa
  Prison Industries, I saved and
  invested these wages in the stock market. These
  investments are currently worth more than
  $12,000 — money I will use to build my life upon release if
  commutation of my sentence, is
  given one day.

- Completed all offered treatment programming by the
  Iowa DOC, including Anger
  Management, Beyond Criminal Thinking, Victim
  Impact, and Primary Chemical
  Dependency.

- Completed the InnerChange Freedom Initiative Program —
  an intensive 18-month, faith-
  based program sponsored by prison fellowship.

Michael E. Blackwell, Sr. #0060156

To Whom It May Concern:

I am 51 years old. I am currently in my 30th year of two consecutive life sentences for murder.

When I came to prison in 1991, I was a lost, angry, and bitter young man. I was still reeling from the murder of my grandfather in 1984, and the dumping of my mother's body in the basement stairwell of an abandoned apartment building in 1987. She had laid there for two days. These tragedies do not justify my actions, but they facilitated my decision to not care anymore. In my anger and bitterness, I became a lying, conniving, selfish, violent, and unforgiving person.

Upon my arrival to prison, I adopted the prison mentality: complained, hated staff, joined a gang, and always blamed someone else for my decisions and actions. My relentless pursuit to fit in commenced a battle within me I labelled, "Life Inside (prison) vs. Life Inside (me), because the two were diametrically opposed to one another. Unfortunately, I chose conformity over transformation and spent the first nine years of my sentence living a lie.

In 2000 something changed inside me. I started thinking more and more about the future; what I would do with a second chance, and I envisioned myself living a changed life. I was compelled to start living it while in prison. Although I did not understand where these thoughts were originating from, I embraced them.

The next 12 years were a transition period for me. I made some mistakes and bad decisions along the way - I still do sometimes -but I am committed to the process. I still am. Escaping a negative mindset is the hardest thing I've ever done. I worked on changing reacting to responding and listening to understand and not always to rebut. I learned that every negative encounter with another race is not always racism, and that the way I carry myself has a lot to do with how people treated me. I came to understand that my attitude had a lot to do with my altitude.

I am now firmly rooted in the positive mindset and growing upward.

In 2008 I founded Humble King Ministries at the Newton Correctional Facility (NCF). In 2013, I started a chapter of Humble King here at the Anamosa State Penitentiary (ASP). When I transferred to the Iowa Medical & Classification Center (IMCC) at Oakdale in 2017, I learned that almost six thousand people had attended Humble King in Anamosa. Upon my arrival at IMCC, I immediately joined the Writer's Workshop. I also joined the Oakdale Choir, headed by Dr. Mary Cohen. I was one of 32 Incarcerated Individuals to be a student of the University of Iowa's Liberal Arts Beyond Bars (LABB) program from its inception, where I maintained a 3.62 GPA. I was also one of three Incarcerated Individuals approved to mentor juvenile Incarcerated Individuals housed at IMCC.

In 2018, I founded, and designed, a three-phase mentoring program called Negative2Positive. I was the first Incarcerated Individual to found a program and make it my job. I designed a logo, put it on shirts, and was allowed to sell them to other Incarcerated Individuals and our families, correctional officers, health care workers, University of Iowa faculty and students, and volunteers. Part of the proceeds were donated to various charities or organizations. I also founded the "Speak Your Truth" poetry event, where the public, as well as, our families, were allowed to come into the institution and participate in an open mic poetry night with us. I have enclosed a Negative2Positive/Speak Your Truth brochure.

No matter what happens at my upcoming Commutation hearing(s), I have dedicated my life to the service of mentoring. I turned in a proposal back in March to start a Negative2Positive program here and am awaiting approval or denial. Upon release, I plan to take Negative2Positive global, and do my part in eliminating negative mindsets.

Thank you for the opportunity to share my journey.
Peace & Balance.

Steve Tryon

This question was recently directed my way: " What changes have you made since your incarceration?"
For me the best way to answer this is to start from the beginning. I started using at the age of 11. Alcohol at first and then adding drugs at the age of 14. But at the same time, I had good parents who did try and teach me right from wrong.

Here was the rub for me, and I suppose for many others. When we are kids and still think the world revolves around us, selfishness and immaturity go hand in hand. Having said that, we are also very aware of what is acceptable and what is not. Drugs and alcohol help quiet the inner voice that tells us to stop- that is unacceptable behavior. So, what we learn is how to ignore our inner voice through addiction.

I believe this is why so many drug and alcohol counselors teach that when you begin using, that is the maturity level you stay at, until sobriety can be obtained. It is only then that your brain can continue to mature and catch you up with your peers, maturity wise.

Again- for me this was a long drawn out process of denial and conflict. At this point I just want to give thanks for a family that did not waiver in their belief that I can get better.

I have now been clean and sober for over 25 years. **(And This Is The Number One Change I Have Made!)** The early years were the hardest. Making the decision to let go of all the people I had been surrounding myself with and finding men with the same hopes for the future was hard. Probably the hardest part of my recovery. In the beginning I read everything I could get my hands on about addiction and addicts. At one point I even authored a couple of pamphlets on addiction. It was also through this time frame that I had begun working with wood in the hobby shop. For the first time in my life I was finishing projects that I'd started. Being a man of my word took on real meaning.

More than anything else, it was a time that I was living my life free of the restraints of addiction.
By the restraints of addiction I mean to say- a small worldly view. Consumed by addiction there
is no room for any kind of real growth. Without these restraints my conscience cleared up. I no longer needed to quiet the inner voice, because I wasn't doing anything that needed to be silenced.

Stanley L. Hart III

<u>"The Responsibility and Remorse Collection"</u>
A Restorative Justice Effort

By Stanley L. Hart III

July 2006

72 hours after turning 18 years old, I murdered my aunt, Marilyn Hart. I am both responsible and remorseful for this terrible crime -- I have been paying my debt to society.

"The Responsibility & Remorse Collection" is an artistic medium to profess responsibility and to express remorse for murdering my aunt. [Written on the back of each picture; numbered and signed.

For murdering my aunt, I bear the greatest burden possible for restorative justice. I cannot return the precious life that I took from her. I cannot repair the horrible damage done to my cousins and to all the other people I victimized by my crime. I can and do accept responsibility. I can and do express the great remorse I experience. These words alone are not enough. My words must be substantiated with actions.

I spent over two decades pursuing rehabilitative opportunities to demonstrate that I reject both my criminal thoughts and the consequent criminal actions. I wanted my actions to speak louder than any words I could say. Those rehabilitative actions, while meaningful and substantial, were not enough. I had to do more.

I wrote apology letters to: my cousins, family church, trial judge, prosecutors, defense lawyers, IA & IL sheriffs, elected federal officials, and the parents of my co-defendants. While meaningful and important, those apology letters were not enough. I had to do more.

I turned my stippling past-time into a continuing gesture of atonement as part of a restorative justice effort. I created an initial commemorative collection as an artistic medium to profess responsibility and to express remorse. That collection began with volume one dedicated to the benefit of my cousins. The collection continued with volume two dedicated to individuals familiar with my crime. The collection concluded with volume three dedicated to public donations. After more than two years of continuous effort, that collection contained 100 pictures. I had to do more.

The Book of James instructs that, "Even so faith, if it has no works, is dead, being by itself. But someone may well say, 'You have faith and I have works; show me your faith without the works, and I will show you my faith by my works'" (2:17-18). I was showing my responsibility and my remorse with each picture completed.

My responsibility and my remorse continue to be demonstrated through "The Responsibility & Remorse Collection" — an artistic medium to profess responsibility and to express remorse for murdering my aunt. Each picture demonstrates my continuing contrition while contributing a meaningful and enduring restorative justice effort to the community.

Uriyel

I greet you in peace and humility. My legal name is Travon Jones. My Iowa inmate number is 6984624. I was requested to right to you and give a summary of accomplishments and a narrative on life changes I have made from the time when my incarceration began 6 long years ago, but before I get into that I will let you know me, the man and the life I lived before my exile from the wonderful life of citizenship.

I am a cousin, nephew, and uncle to my very own family and last but definitely not least, a better father to those two beautiful Queens in process.

Aside from an educational and self-help standpoint, I also have had an enormous spiritual growth while incarcerated as well. Even as a small child, I was not ignorant to the flagrant differences between **the** people who looked like me and the people who did not look like me, which led me to believe that I must not mean as much to society as a brother or sister who may, by chance, have as small as a difference in appearance as having a lighter skin complexion than me. But through my spiritual journey I found out that we should not be judged by the complexion of our skin, the social class we identify with or even where we live in the world whether a person was forced there or made the conscious decision to live self-building groups such as A.V.P. has helpful

My intentions after starting my music-oriented company was to show and help as many youths from my community as I could to have a better life through legal means. As a result I invited a handful of young inspiring artist and representatives to join my company so that we could build something wonderful. As a result of this I was placed in a misfortunate situation which landed me in prison with a 171/2 year mandatory, away from life, away from freedom, and most importantly, away from my family.

As dangerous as a storm as this seems to the reader for me to traverse through, there was silver lining within the dark clouds that obnoxiously lingered over head and I will tell you why; From the moment I breached the giant, barb wired equipped metal gate, (a representation of self-restriction and physical bondage), I refused to let my mind be caged into a box, because I knew if I gave up on my mind, I would consequently give up on my body and my soul which as I learned from the nurturing teachings of my mother, grandmother, great grandmother and all my ancestors who came is not an option. This mindset passed on from generation to generation lead se my mind through reading non-fictional, informational books, aimed at ng process and opening up a person's mind to a variety of ways of living and body may be have always been seen as a leader amongst my peers, I was just a little rough around the edges, but while being in prison I never fail to take the opportunities given by the state to better myself. This has not only led me to complete one C.A.L.M. group but also obtain three awards for a nationally recognized group called A.V.P. (Alternative to Violence Program). Not only have I received recognitions for participation, I took it one step further and made the conscience decision to lead this nationally renowned group as what we call a 'Facilitator' of the chapter that operates here in the Iowa State Penitentiar0Seing a facilitator-of eater and allow for my part to er confronted with aggressive or confrontational individual 2) Communicate peoples and personalities which I had previously not have even dared to deal with before 3) To empathize with why and how someone feels in a particular moment and 4) Become a better leader which in turn teaches me to be a better teacher to anyone with ears, a better brother, son, have alternative Opti with where they chose to live because our Creator loves us equally and only wants the best for mankind. No matter what spiritual background you identify with you will consistently see that whoever looks down on us, when he wants to speak to us, he calls us by <u>Name.</u> He does not call us by color, He does not call us by what part of the city we live in, and He does not call us depending on how much money we have in our pocket. Understanding this will not solve all the problems in the world, but it will begin the painstaking process of changing the mindset of people who don't understand, just as it has done for me.

I will now leave you with Peace, Love and Wisdom.

You know me as Travon Jones #6984624

My spiritual name is Uriyel

Editors note: Uriel included a signed, notarized affidavit, hand written by his co-defendant, Mr. Darrion Morrisey, stating that Travon had no knowledge of what was going to happen and did not participate in any of the crimes he was convicted of. Mr. Morrisey states he has informed to DA of this and is willing to testify to these facts.

August 1st 2020

Eid Nassif

My name is Eid Nassif inmate at Iowa State Prison. I have been in prison since 1990 as of September 1st. I came to prison when I was just 21 years old as a young adult I didn't understand the things I did and now I have 30 years in I came to Ft. Madison Iowa State prison and my journey began. It was then I had to decide what to make of myself my whole life is gone, and I had life without parole at such a young age for the shooting death of another young adult. I started out working and taking programs my first job, I worked as a barber and then started a plumber job with the plumbing apprenticeship after I finished that I started The HVACs apprenticeship. I have held jobs from kitchen worker to medical orderly and now work for IPI Iowa Prison Industry making cabinets for habitat for humanity and I am taking the apprenticeship for that I also have helped out with creating barber worksheets for the prisons were it will allow others to take their apprenticeships. I have been report free and get along with staff and others I have enclosed some certificates and generic notes by staff showing my good conduct. I also held positions as the president for the NAACP and took my ADLA certificate helping the older inmates during hospice I also do SSIP which I watch inmates that are in a cell that are trying to hurt them self's or others. I have been a mentor to the younger inmates. I also took thinking for change and Avp I have been to other prisons in Iowa and have held the same jobs .As a lifer without parole I would like to have others just hear my story my dad went to prison in 1987 and at that time I was 17 years old I didn't have a good life and started to use drugs which caused me to meet others that sold or used drugs and then that lead to me having problems and caused the crime I am here for. I have not had no fights or any drug use since I been in prison, I did obtain a few reports during my time in prison but nothing that caused harm to others. I have married Elli Nassif which has been by my side and still is to this day. Now I am 51 years old and still hold on to faith that one day the law will change and give myself and others a second chance as my brain developed and I started to understand the life I lived and now living I am not the same person as I was at 21 years old I am trying to go to another prison but do to the COVID 19 that is been put on hold. I have high hopes and will keep the faith that people will see as a young adult are brains was still developing and decision making was not there for good reasons. Thank you for listening to my story.

Eid Nassif

Summary of **Cedric B. Theus**

Before I begin to speak about my journey, and growth, I must acknowledge the victim in my case. His name is Terranee-Gibsett. He was 19 years old and I took his future from him. His family and friends went through a trauma that no family should ever have to endure. My views and experience of how my life has changed or is in no way meant to infer that I should not have to suffer consequences for the events that took place the night of Terrance's death. I simply want to show that today I am not same person I was back then.

On March 13th, 1996 I was an 18 year old father of 2 who was addicted to alcohol. I lived in Sioux City at the time. After my kids' mother caught me with another woman, the ex-girlfriend of my victim's friend, she and I had a huge argument. She threatened to take our kids and move to another state because she was fed up with my drinking and cheating. I felt like my life was over. I had recently lost my job at UPS due to a back injury, and was barely attending classes at Western Iowa Tech.

In spite of my addiction and flaws as a boyfriend, I loved being a father. I couldn't imagine life without my babies. I seriously contemplated ending my life. I was very intoxicated on the night of the argument with my girlfriend and needed immediate help. My kids' mother talked me out of killing myself and into getting help. She knew that there were underlying issues that I needed professional help to deal with. There was no place for me to go for in-patient treatment in Sioux City that I could find. On March 14, I called a facility in Sioux Falls, SD. They agreed to help me with my addiction, depression, and childhood trauma issues. A bus ticket to Sioux Falls would be waiting for me around 7am on March 15th. The treatment center would be waiting for me once I arrived. I felt hopeful for the first time in a while. My father was a Marine Corps veteran, so I had plans of entering the Marine Corps as a second lieutenant after I earned my degree. I decided on the 14th that I wouldn't wait to finish school. Once I finished treatment I would enlist in the Marine Corps and become the man that I knew I could be.

Unfortunately, instead of boarding a bus to Sioux Falls on the morning of March 15th, I was booked into the Woodbury County jail for first-degree felony murder. A few hours earlier I had taken the life of a 19 year old man after a verbal dispute with his friend and subsequent altercation with him when he became involved. The victim, and I had be on bad terms from him becoming upset at his then girl friend at a party.

On the night of the shooting, I thought it was a good idea to have some drinks, at my girlfriend's home, for one last time before I would likely have to give up alcohol for the foreseeable future. Although I wasn't so drunk that I couldn't function, I made a series of decisions that I would've never made sober.

I am not blaming the alcohol, Terrance, or anyone else for my choices. I just want to give you some context regarding my mentality in 1996 and some of the circumstances surrounding my crime. I am 100% responsible for my actions that night.

Since that night, I have had 24½ years to reflect on my mistakes and poor choices. Each day I endeavor show myself and my family that I am more than the worst thing I have ever done. Before prison, I was a broken and hopeless individual who didn't understand that each choice I make affects not only my life, but the lives of so many others. I have developed a level of empathy and compassion for other's that I never had when I was younger. My journey has caused my thoughts to shift from believing that it's alright to do wrong and violate certain laws out of necessity to vowing not to break the law again because the consequences are not worth it, to now believing that crime is a violation of myself, others, and society. Necessity and fear of consequence no longer cloud my view of crime. Restorative justice has helped me realize that I have an obligation to my victims, myself, my family and community for the harms that I have caused. I understand the true impact of all crimes from something as simple as speeding and other "minor" crimes, to violent acts that cause physical, emotional, and psychological harms. My life is now guided by restorative values that are free of violence, fear, manipulation, and the option of committing crime.

I have learned to love myself and can now love humanity. Love has also caused me to be more cognizant of the harms that humans cause to animals and the planet— and I feel have an obligation to be just to both. I can now see littering, or killing insects unnecessarily, as a harm and violation of my true essence. I am dedicated to giving back to my family and society by making positive decisions.

Carlos Robinson

Same person...

Let me start off by saying "I haven't changed a bit in the last 20 years of my incarceration." I would like to believe I am the same person I was the day I was removed from the streets and up and until even now 20 years later. I would like to believe my attitude on life was and is still the same as it was when they snatched away from my life with the four babies that I and their mother conceived (the family life) and forced me to walk through the doors of penitentiary life. I told myself even then I had two years or less and I would be back with those I loved the most. Since I've been here, I've had women come and go. I've had my babies write to me and send pictures. I even had a sprinkle of family visits to make times a little better. After all that, I still would like to believe I am the same person I was when I was forced to walk through the doors of penitentiary life.

Being here showed me the reasons why people should never break the law. Being here told me that if I wasn't criminally minded before, I would be now. This place, the penitentiary life shows you the ins and outs of how to be the best criminal, the best slick talker, the best hustler and the best tough talker a man could ever be and who would want to leave all that?

Since I've been here, I would like to believe I am still the same person I was twenty years ago...but I am not. Because I was starting to see what others saw in me that landed me in this situation, I grew away from the boy I used to be into a man I needed to be. I now think before I react. I now immerse myself in self-help activities so I can help the incoming class which seems to be getting younger and younger by the year. I've always wanted to be an educator and even though I was unable to finish my dream of being the best teacher, educator in the world, I still have those aspirations and on occasion employ them as needed.

Being in prison is definitely not the place I want to be and I would not wish this on my worst enemy however, maybe this was the place I needed to be to realize that I was not headed down the right path from the beginning. This most definitely was and is a wakeup call that allows me to create my own destiny. I ask myself, "Do I ever want to leave this place, or do I want to make this prison my home?" Because of the man I have become over the years, I now realize what is most important to me and that is to have the love I so longingly hoped for. To be surrounded with my children and now grandchildren. I now take nothing for granted anymore. I know now at any given time or day, I could be there at home with family which was/is the best place to be to in the blink of an eye being here with those that do not have my best interests at heart. Even though I was 29 when I was arrested, I know now I was still a kid, a child in a man's body who didn't put away childish things. It shouldn't have taken for me to be removed from family life and up to twenty years to realize this however, the lesson was learned and now the ultimate question is what do I do to rectify this? How do I put myself in a position to get back to what I wanted since I was fifteen years of age? The answer is, to not be the same person I was the day I was removed from the streets and forced to walk through the doors of penitentiary life.

John Epps

My Name is John Epps, and I have been incarcerated since 1998. Some guards have noticed the quality of character that I have. This has come as a result of internal work I have been committed to change. My case is first degree murder. Iowa law is unforgiving for such a crime. I understand that and don't complain about the law. I have only sought those that have the power to grant clemency. I have acquired my GED since being incarcerated, and numerous of vocational diplomas. I serve as a mentor on behavioral improvements.

When a person violates laws it not only affects them, but it affects others. Humanity has been endowed with power to serve others, bringing happiness to those who that I facilitate a Hebrew Roots teaching class three times per week. This allows prisoners that desire a deep inner change to find the source of that change. I call this a TBR (Torah Base Program). The Torah is the Hebrew for "instruction." Instruction on how to live a restored life is within the Torah. In 2005, Governor Vilsack heard an application filed by me for clemency. he had noticed maturity, and the great change of attitude, but he declined the clemency. There was consolation in his words of my change. This is what have wanted even though I didn't receive clemency. I did receive an inner release and continue toward change. There are some men that have been incarcerated for life and have a vision of being somebody. They want the opportunity to do so.

When power is abused it causes others to suffer. This abuse sometimes leads to incarceration. The attempt is to rehabilitate the offender of the law. The question must be asked, "Does imprisonment rehabilitate lawbreakers?" This article's objective is not to malign the criminal justice system or prison administrators. Rather, the objects is to focus on the effects of prison and whether rehabilitation is truly possible through Correctional Systems.

As a person serving life for first degree murder, I believe I have an expertise on this subject. I've personally experienced what prison can and cannot do for lawbreakers.

Committing crimes is a result of not having empathy for others. When prisoners begin to have empathy they are on their way toward rehabilitation. I am writing this from my own experience of incarceration. I began to accept the responsibility for my wrong actions. I stopped making excuses or blaming the external for wrong behavior. The problem wasn't external it was internal.

Anonymous Lifer

Lips of Blue

We don't have the Death Sentence in Iowa: REALLY?

"Iowa a Place to Grow"

This is the State of Iowa motto, stamped on our vehicle license plates that are pounded out by Iowa prisoners, painted on our highway signs welcoming visitors from out of and into our state, worn on t-shirts, spoken at rallies and functions of every kind, printed on buttons worn on lapels, taught to our children, These are the words that Iowans proudly represent.

Let's speak first and foremost about the victims in these entire matters, the victims and their families, my immediate family, my personal family, the community and the State of Iowa. The actions caused by me to everyone has been devastating to say the least for which I am truly sorry and sincerely apologize.

Continuing

Four decades and change this has been my life. Chosen by me, a horrible choice, an irresponsible choice, deserving by law, deserving of consequences via my own actions. No excuses offered, none rendered, no alibis, just the truth and nothing but the truth.

The punishment meted out and levied upon my soul for the balance of my natural life. Welcome to confinement — from this very real moment of day 1 of incarceration there will never be any such consideration for me by the State of Iowa via any type of redemption, transformation, just dues of any sorts, time served other than to its fullest as stated in my first administrative/resident notice received whereby it states in bold red capital letters: **Date of discharge? AT DEATH!** Signed by Ms. Debbie Nichols ISP Administrative Assistant and stamped with the ISP Warden's Signature affirming such notice of delivery.

Fast forward a decade and $^1/_2$. Commutation Hearing — Denied — Severity. Again fast forward 7 years: Commutation Hearing — Denied — Severity. Again, fast forward **5** years: Commutation Hearing — Denied — Severity.

My file continues to reveal but a snapshot of my past and they are so uninterested in my incarcerated past and present status, my character, compassion's, and services to the very community I offended.

Listen

You could hear a pin drop, but you cannot hear a word I am saying. You are blinded by the injustices you as an agent of Iowa are causing to hundreds of lifers serving LWOP. Truth is, you are not deaf to the cries for reformation as pleaded for by me and other lifers of Iowa you just refuse to see it in any light. I (we) are not asking for the Governor or its agents to free all lifers, rather, I (we) are asking for the fundamental fairness to be offered in my commutation reviews for redemption and/or clemency to those of us who have shown change in our lives since my/our incarceration(s).

If we peel back the layers and reveal the true rancid smell of the states "Lex Talionis" and its spoils I (we) are labeled as minimizing and/or non-remorseful. The fact is, there is no remorse for decades of cruel and unusual punishment by the state or its agents, there is no compassion for the lifer who has given his or her final declaration of remorse and have done the right thing since our incarcerations. The state continues to serve its dough balls of "HOPE" that will lay in the bellies of the beasts. It's quite simple they've been nothing other than our bloated balls of denial for clemency — DENIED — Severity.

The Boards Decision of Severity

Compared to What? Or Whose Crime? Or Whose Age? Or Whose Length of Time Served?

I (we) beseech you to refrain from relying upon and viewing these past 40 plus years and the prejudicial "Snapshot" for your reasoning of your decision-making for my continued confinement. Rather, look forward to the Transformation for Hope, the Remorse and Compassion of today. Provide me the modicum of my fundamental fairness at my/our hearings with truth in meaning and compassion coupled with the Due Process Standards.

Some of us, not all, have endured hardships of our own — not specifically us but that of our own families who've traveled down this Road of Despair. They too have been given the LWOP. They too have become victims of this continued incarceration, provide them with long overdue mercy and forgiveness and free them from this LWOP.

I can write or beg until I am blue in the face — But wait, my lips have turned blue already remember? It is the result from the decades of "Death by Strangulation" from the ropes of injustices levied at my clemency hearings.

We're still swinging from Iowa's Gallows. Don't leave us hanging here, we're not Mussolini. We too find it difficult to breathe with this rope around our necks. It's time to review our incarcerated past. Now there's a SNAPSHOT!

However, the geographic location of being in the **Bible Belt** of this country, where we pray and attest for forgiveness's and mercy we continue to be "Iowa a place to Grow" (Old in Prison) We do not Forget or Forgive. **And Proud of It!!!**

<u>Once Again Listen</u>

The Gallows trap door has opened again for at least the 76oth time.

It is time to show Compassion and Mercy at our Clemency Hearings as they have been intended and designed to provide to those who ARE worthy of a Second Chance at LWP and a society release. Our law books say so right?

Signed,

Just Hanging around Dangling and Twitchin'

Ramale Hunt

We as people have all the forces of good within the universe in us. We too have all the forces of bad within the universe in us. These forces are simply positive and negative energy. The key to life is to embrace the positive and suppress the negative. There is a thin line that separates the two and that is the power of choice. With this power of choice we can choose to embrace positive or negative energy in any and every situation in life. This isn't a concept I knew of or even can say I would have agreed to when I was out in the free world. However, it is a concept I chose to adopt within the first few years of my incarceration.

I chose to adopt this concept because I knew it was a negative lifestyle that led me to prison so it would take a positive outlook to overcome it. I wanted to be more than the negative labels that were being placed on me. Really it wasn't about me it was about my son. I wanted to be better for him. I didn't want him growing up viewing me on my past transgressions. I didn't want him to see the streets as an option for his life. It was time for me to revolutionize my ways for the better and that started with positive thinking. I promised myself that I would surround myself around positive people and that I would involve myself in positive outlets. I wanted my thoughts to be pure and positive and my words and actions to be intended to create good. "What good are one's words if they don't provoke positive thought and action".

People grow as their knowledge grows so my promise led me to self-help groups such as Alternative to Violence Project (AVP), Project Harmony, NAACP, Toastmasters and Humanism. All of these groups have been tremendously helpful in my maturation process and I've become very instrumental in all of them however AVP has given me the most tangible tools to deal with daily life. AVP has what is called the 12 guides to "Transforming Power" which are ways for you to tap into positive energy and allow you the ability to alternate or enhance any situation for the better. I've gained communication skills, relationship skills and conflict resolution skills. I've gained empathy which has become one of my greatest qualities. Being able to truly empathize has given me insight and understanding on victims and victims' families' pain, even my family's pain as well. It's a quality that everyone should embrace. I've also gained knowledge and understanding on trauma, grief, guilt, self-esteem and anger. I've learned better ways to parent from prison and what restorative justice is and how to use it. This is just some and not all the things that I've gained from AVP.

AVP pretty much covers any situation in life so I honestly believe I have gained the knowledge to help me through any situation life may throw at me. It has been very vital with my relationship with my son. Everything I've learned I apply it to him, and it has helped us form a great bond. I even became an AVP facilitator so I can help others gain all that I have gained from AVP. I owe a great deal of my growth to our lead facilitator known to us as "Smiling Sandy". Sometimes the student is only as good as the teacher, well for me I had a great teacher. Without her dedication, commitment and love I don't think I would have grown as much as I have. She sees us as more than the negative labels that were placed on us, she seen us as our authentic spiritual selves. I genuinely love her like a mother. AVP challenged me to do better, to

be better, and to have humility. It changed me and gave me perspective and for that I live my life by this Thomas Paine quote; "The world is my country and to do good is my religion".

My promise to myself also led me to the <u>Moorish Science Terrual of America.</u> The M.S.T. of A. is a school of thought it teaches us to live our lives according to the 5 highest divine principles known to man which are Love, Truth, Peace, Freedom and Justice. By doing so we are living up to the true essence of the word Islam which is our hands, tongue and thoughts do not hurt others. The goal of a man's life according to Islam is peace with everything. Peace with God and peace with man. We are taught that everyone has within him the seed of perfect development and it rests solely with himself to make or mar his fortune. These are beliefs that I hold to be true, beliefs that I model my life after.

The M.S.T. of A. also teaches us the concept of the Higher and Lower self which brought me full circle with positive and negative energy. The Higher self (spirit in man/positive energy) is the Mother of virtues and the harmonies of life, and breeds Justice, Mercy, Love and Right. The Lower self (physical man/negative energy) sometimes called the "Devil" breeds

Hatred, Slander, Lewdness, Murder, Theft and everything that harms. The Higher self is everything that the Lower self is not; it is our authentic spiritual self. This self, the Higher self is what I strive to be.

It is thoughts and a man's character that dictates his conduct.

Bruce Lee once said that any knowledge gained ultimately is self-knowledge. Knowledge gives you perspective; it changes you for the better. I'm on a never-ending quest for knowledge of self. On that quest I will continue to live by the concept of the Higher and Lower self and the ability to embrace positive energy in any situation in life. I will also continue to live by the 5 highest divine principles known to man which are Love, Truth, Peace, Freedom and Justice. With this as my foundation I can only be righteous in all my acts, words, and deeds. Peace

-Ramale A. Hunt-El

Christina Shepard

At 20 years of age, after 3 and one-half years of physical and emotional abuse at the hands of my husband and father of my son, I murdered my abuser. It was 1990 when I was sentenced to Life With Out Parole. I have been incarcerated for 20 years now.

When I first came to prison, I searched for meaning---how could someone like myself, a pacifist who loves all living things and wouldn't harm a bug, have killed another human being? It took years of studying psychology and intense therapy to come to terms the fact that I took a life. The shame and guilt I still feel is overwhelming, and in the beginning, it incapacitated me. But I am a fighter, determined to find my way back to the person I was before I met my victim.

I was 15 in 1983. We lived in the country and my parents were overprotective evangelicals. They would not let me date until I was 16. I think it is fair to say I was naïve. My plan was to graduate high school and go to college. Kevin was out of school. My parents met him and let him come to the house supervised, but they did not like him. For many reasons I now understand I continued seeing him and at 16 I found myself pregnant. I considered alternatives to the pregnancy but decided to keep the baby. My son was born when I was 17 and I felt the greatest sense of joy and love I have ever felt.

There were many signs of Kevin's violent tendencies which I did not recognize as warning signs. I was too inexperienced at life when it was happening. I was raised to believe the nuclear family is a priority in life, so I stayed. He beat me when he couldn't control me, and he was very jealous/possessive. On three occasions I picked up a knife to fight back. I called the police on several occasions and I was hospitalized on a psychiatric unit several times for suicidal attempts.

Since being incarcerated I have learned about my poor decision-making skills, and because my brain still had plasticity upon entering the prison, I was an ideal candidate for rehabilitation. Those errant and poor decision makings I experienced before are no longer a part of my psychological make-up. I still make mistake at 51, but I use the lessons from those mistakes to adjust my perceptions and behavior in beneficial ways. I have volunteered through the Iowa Coalition Against Domestic Abuse for seminars at ICIW, sand intend to further my community involvement helping victims like myself upon release. I am currently finishing an associate degree through Des Moines Area Community College (DEMACC) affiliated with the Skylark Project to empower women to be independent, and therefore less vulnerable to the risk of abuse. I will continue to achieve aa bachelor's degree. I am an active member of Kiwanis, sponsored through the Altoona Iowa Chapter of Kiwanis. I presently volunteer for the ICIW dog program, P.A.W.S. Many of our dogs get placed with Veterans in need. I have a fulltime job for Iowa Prison Industries as an Administrative Clerk in the Plastics Department. I sincerely regret the pain and suffering I have caused others by committing homicide. I cannot take it back or change it. If I would have taken the plea bargain offered me in 1989, I would have been sentenced to 6-8 years because it was a domestic violence case.

David Foell

August 10, 2020

My Name is David, 0082130, and I am a Lifer at Iowa State Penitentiary. I believe in second chances. I came to the DOC in 1991 upon arrest for the first charge ever on my clean file in my whole life. Until I was arrested December 9, 1991, I only had a driving record where I admit I did drink alcohol first and second and two driving under suspension charges. So, yes, I was using alcohol back in my youth at 15 years of age into adulthood. So since I came into DOC June 5, 1992 I have chosen to make positive changes in my life to change myself so that one day I can get that second chance that I believe I have earned or achieved. Here is a summary of changes I made over the years in prison.

1992-2020:

I signed up for prison Fellowship Seminary's, two a year, one in Spring and one in the Fall from 1992 – 1997. I received two certificates per years for those 5 years. In 1992 I also signed up for Alcohol Awareness Program and went through parts one and two. I still attend aftercare. I also attended Bible Study until the ACLU filed a suit and closed it down. I got certificates for all these also.

I also have had jobs like lumper job and janitor work here in prison. I have life skills in Upholstery School run by Mike Petersen who retired in 2004-05. So, I also worked in the kitchen various jobs like food server and prep cook and dish room and pots and pans. I have worked at Iowa Prison Industries, jobs like seal sander and lumper job Unit Two until I was moved.

I signed up for apprenticeship program for Housekeeping in 2018, and I graduated on which is a life skill for an employer upon release of re-entry to society. I signed up for Toastmaster's in February 2019 to present where I am a member and have served in several jobs within monthly meetings which gives me a platform for speaking skills.

I have been a member of the Alcohol Awareness Program/meeting on Monday's. I take part and I lead whatever capacity I am asked to do monthly to read and to open and to share from my past experiences of alcohol ordeals. I took the program and am now a member of the aftercare group. All this is beneficial to me and to others in their situations. Also, I am in Project Harmony, a group which meets monthly on Tuesday. We are a diverse group that share cultures and videos on our different cultures. I have also signed up for Alternative to Violence ATV) classes and the self-esteem courses.

I graduated from both ATV and Self Esteem and I received two awards from those programs. I have taken Thinking for A Change classes which is 26 sessions and I graduated from that program also. I continue to go to support group run by Lynn on Tuesday's.

I recently signed up for M.R.I.T. which is run by Dan Roach of Iowa Prison Industries. It is a 13-week course, and I will get a certificate when I am done.   I have recently contacted the Education Department to see about taking classes, but it is on hold because of COVID.

So, yes, I made a TERRIBLE mistake in my life and I regret what I did and I live with it every day. I am now trying to make amends here in DOC to try and get a second change to re-enter society. I want to try to get a second chance to start over an to take care of my only family member left, my mom. So, to achieve it all, yes, we make progress slow steps, but it is slow steps we attain small goals each year in DOC. I do believe in second chance for me and for others in DOC.

Thank you for listening to me.

Imere Hall

I am Imere Hall, a 22-year-old African American man sentenced to Life With Out Parole 4 years ago at age 18. I was sentenced as a participant in a murder, robbery, **not** as the shooter, but for being there and refusing to testify against a co-defendant and refusing a plea deal. I am responsible for my part in the crime.

Since I've been incarcerated, I received my Hi-Set/GED on December 14, 2019. I have completed a Basic Industrial Maintenance Tech college course and received 9 Endorsements. Currently I am accepted to the Forklift course and am just waiting for the classes to start. I will be taking the Alternative to Violence classes and Thinking For A Change also.

I have not received a major report in all 4 years and have not been in the hole. I have maintained a job 2 of the 3 years here in prison. Some would like to say I am a model inmate, just trying to get back to his family. I am doing everything I can to someday get back to my family. I have two girls, ages 6 and 3.

Jason Hiveley

To summarize what I have done to better myself and my way of thinking since I've been incarcerated, I have:

Gotten my GED; been trained in "Lexus Nexis" law library training, taken Silican training dealing with hazardous airborne materials working in Maintenance, "Lock Out, Tag Out: training; and worked in Maintenance for 15+ years.

I have taken and completed "Thinking For a Change"; completed "Alternatives To Violence" to learn how to handle feelings and behavior.

I have applied for 3 different college courses that have been offered, 2 electrical training and 1 pumps and valves training, but none of that is happening now because of the COVID virus.

I am currently working at Iowa Prison Industries in the Habitat for Humanity department and will be starting the cabinetry apprenticeship program.

Along a personal view, I am interested in living a family life of peace and quiet, growing old and hopefully being able to steer people away from the wrong paths in life. Interestingly, life does not have to be drugs and partying.

Travis Wolfkill

When it comes to the subject of positive transformation, I find it is best to not talk about the subject. To address those who still desire a certain lifestyle is to speak to your own past. They either can't hear you or they will not. The best way is to show them.

Some prefer the expression, "lead by example." The thing is you don't have to lead. The journey is personal. Just be about the journey. Then you will find too much discussion is unproductive.

- journal entry, 10.17.20

"The Jewels"

One of the most precious pieces of advice I found inside is, "Know Yourself."

This automatically appealed to me because it is universal. It is not cut from the cloth of a particular religious tradition. It does not originate from politics, academia, or even fortune cookies. This advice is a gem I want to share with you, seekers of reason and progress.

Your birthday- known in the old world as one's feast day. Contrary to popular belief, not everyone knows their actual date of birth. I knew a Sudanese refugee who explained that many of his brothers and sisters had the official D.O.B. of "January 1". The UN did not have complete records when these children were taken from parts of war-torn Africa.

I was born on Friday the 13th. In the 80's and 90's this would get more of a reaction than it does today. I finally researched the issue while in prison. It turns out Friday the 13th is considered an "unlucky" or cursed day because of the legendary Knights Templar. Their Order was falsely accused and arrested on that dark day in October of 1307.

Your birthstone- I used to think this was something mainly women were interested in. A much younger inmate recently asked me if I knew what my birthstone is. It was a little humbling to admit I did not. I couldn't even register a guess. Being a science enthusiast and I didn't know about certain stratified gems... After reading basic reference materials I now know what sardonyx is. It is rare, like me.

Your name- William Shakespeare is the one who gets credit for the famous line, "A rose by any other name is still a rose." I believe the Bard was on the right track but the wrong train. Our name is very important. The name we were given by our family. The one we prefer to be called and of course the one we have earned.

I have earned the respect to be addressed as a human being. I am not an "offender" and I don't feel the need to wear the title, "incarcerated individual." I am a man and a student of nature and self. I realized that long term incarceration is inhumane. My empathy won't let me ignore this truth.

Once an individual becomes self-aware, it is imperative we begin the process to de-carcerate. This is the philosophy I value, and it helps me rise above the madness of isolation.

Your birthday, your birthstone and your name. These are the jewels we wear. Let us think like kings and queens and elevate our consciousness.

Travis Wolfkill

Jeff Hoover

My name is Jeffrey Hoover. I am 51 years old. In 1985 at the age of 21 I was sentenced to Life With Out Parole for kidnapping and robbery.

I have been here for 35 years. I have not seen the parole board in over 30 years.

I wish to begin by confessing that I take full responsibility for the pain that I have caused so many. Something that I could not have done 35 years ago. I will explain.

But first, please let me say I am extremely humbled in my heart to have the opportunity to tell you about myself. The young man that was sentenced to prison for life and the man I have become today.

When I was sentenced to Life I could not understand why I was given Life. I understood that what I did was wrong, but I did not understand the severity of my crime. I didn't take anyone's life so why was my life being taken from me? That is how I thought and reasoned when I was 21.

I DID NOT KNOW how to empathize with the people I had hurt. Over many years with the help of my wonderful parents, especially my mother. I began not just to understand, but to feel in my heart the severity of the pain I have caused.

That same severity that had escaped me all those years ago, for the first time in my life I felt empathy, true empathy for all those I have hurt in my life. And I welcomed this revelation because to me, that it what it was. With this revelation came regret and shame. But it also began the path that led me to the man I am today.

I cannot go any further without acknowledging Holy Spirit and Jesus without whom I could not have stayed this path all these many years.

I have grown into a man I can respect. A man who thoughtfully thinks and reasons before he acts. I have spent many years mentoring younger men here in prison and I feel I have much to offer.

I have been a cook and baker for over 30 years. I enjoy sharing my knowledge and skills of cooking and baking that many men have taken to the streets when they have gone home.

I participated in "Thinking For A Change" several years ago to help me better understand and change the way I behaved and thought when I was younger. I am now and have been an active member of ATJ---"Alternative to Violence" I enjoy this very much as it gives me an opportunity to be around men that have the same values, goals and aspirations that I have and to help one another to achieve them.

The hope I have is that anyone who sees this will see not the boy I was but the man I have become.

Keith Bruns

I have been incarcerated since April 19, 1979. I was sentenced to LWOP for kidnapping and sexual abuse which occurred in Cedar Falls Iowa in January of 1979. I was 20 years old at the time of the offense. I am now 62 years of age. I have exhausted all avenues of appeal and have no pending legal actions in this matter. I take full responsibility for the crime I committed and am truly regretful for all the suffering, pain and trauma that I have caused to all those who have been affected by my actions. I have profound empathy for all who have been hurt by my actions.

I have been very successful in my rehabilitation efforts. I have no institutional disciplinary problems. I have taken the opportunity afforded me by the Iowa Department of Corrections to grow, increase my education and skill sets as well as become a productive member of the community I reside in. I am a positive model and example that others can follow to better themselves.

Through my employment opportunities I have developed very good problem-solving skills which have made me a productive and trusted worker and leader in the areas I have worked in. These skills have also been instrumental in how I have changed in my decisions that affect others and myself. I am fully aware of any consequences which may follow any decision that I make. I have learned that good consequences follow good choices and are easier for me and others to live with than the things that are associated with negative consequences which occur because of bad choices/decisions.

I have moved to a lead position in all the following work areas:

Metal Shop, Education Department, Medical/Hospice Units, Woodworking School, Wood Shop, Custom Wood Working, Hobby Craft, Furniture making, Sign making, Tire Recapping, Custom Wood and Food store/Commissary.

I have been instrumental in starting new ventures within my assigned work areas, having started two separate woodworking schools with curriculum and three wood shops from scratch with the assistance of others.

I have completed the following apprenticeships and I have obtained Journeyman Status in each of them:

Cabinetmaking, Metal Fabrication, Silk Screening, Structural Painting, Building Maintenance.

I will soon complete my apprenticeship as Office Manager.

Everything I have achieved and been successful at to this point has been with the knowledge that I would surely die in prison. Doing what I have done is the surest indicator that I have changed and am rehabilitated.

Kline Goeders

Just as a stage setter, nothing about this was like television portrays. I remember the day of arrest and the sight of the guns pointed at me was very sobering and the barrels looked huge. Telling my wife at the time what I had been arrested for was so hard to do and there was no sympathy in the room. The first days just flew by in a blur and then the trial was over. The jury was only out for 4 hours. I knew it was not good for me.

When they came into the courtroom, this was the only time I did not stand. I actually couldn't, my knees had turned to jelly. The newspaper article said that I had maintained my composure. There was just nothing I could do physically.

I knew from that time that if I were to ever have any chance for release, I would have to be a model citizen in some of the worst conditions. I was the man that made lemonade from lemons so to speak.

From the first job to the one I am currently in, I always made sure that the job carried responsibility. I was first a cook at the Iowa State Penitentiary (ISP) at Ft. Madison, IA. In upholstery next and transitioned to custom upholstery. I was also on the Prisoner Advisory Council at ISP. I worked my way to the Honor Lifer Range where there were more privileges. I stayed in maximum security for 10 years and then went to John Bennett Unit which was right next to ISP and was medium/maximum security. I stayed there for the next 11 years and again I was in higher profile jobs. Bakery, library, Iowa

Prison Industries (IPI) doing clothes. While there I bagged sandbags for the town of Niota, IL.

While at JBU, I did specialty baking for the visiting room, School Graduations, visiting staff functions. I also became proficient with the computer while there and created a work disk to go with a workbook for Microsoft Word. At the request of the teacher, I also assisted with the New Beginnings class which was a Computer Competence class. I also made a brochure for one of the Old Thresher Days when the printing presses were there. I also volunteered to be one of the first inmate observers for a new program called SSIP- Suicide, Self-Injury Prevention; that was to keep an eye on people who may have intended harm to themselves or others.

I transferred to Mt. Pleasant Correctional Facility in 2008, and again went to jobs with high visibility. Working for Iowa Prison Industries, I was outside the main fence, but still fenced in and held the position of shipping clerk. I also did payroll and worked with the Global program. I worked there until we closed down and then was trained and then worked in Health Services as the only orderly. I was responsible for all the inventory and maintaining a high level of cleanliness.

I transferred to Ft. Dodge Correctional Facility in December of 2010 to be closer to my siblings and for more opportunity. Upon my arrival there, worked in the visiting room as the orderly and picture taker and set up man for the many staff functions in the conference room attached to the visiting room. When a job opportunity in R & D opened up, I took it. There, more responsibility was expected, and it was good for me. I helped with intake of arriving inmates, tagged clothes, etched names and numbers into electronics and Cd's. I was also a Commander of the Veterans Organization, Vice Commander, Treasurer also. The theme for me since my incarceration has been to build trust. I also completed an Alternative To Violence Program basic workshop.

While at FDCF, I became involved with Leader Dog For The Blind and raised 2 puppies for them and cared for a retired Leader Dog for over 7 years till she was put down last November. I was involved with Backpack for Buddies, which packed lunches for school children who did not get proper nutrition on weekends. I have done my best to turn from the man I was when I entered prison to become one who can be trusted with anything. I now work in the kitchen storeroom where I track and distribute inventory as needed. I can do any job in the kitchen without supervision and perform all that I am called to do. I am the current President of the Inside Council for Church of Damascus Road. I have been on the council for almost 5 years now. We support various organizations outside even through this trying time for all people, everywhere. I am currently at the North Central Correctional Facility and have been here for over 3 years.

I believe that if asked or looked into, one might find that many people doing life without parole did their crime by accident. They did not set out to do what they did that day or night. Please accept my thanks for your time and interest in us. All that I have said is open to anyone. Thank you again.

Mark Daryl Becker

My grandfather was 88 when he passed away, and it was in December 2019. I knew him as a smart, humorous to witty person. He also suffered from a brain disease. I know that my brain disease was horrible and his was horrible too. When he got Alzheimer's I was having Schizophrenia, Paranoid Type. When he died, I got, very close to the exact day, photographic memories that my brain had blacked out for 11 years and 9 months. And I became a changed man.

Now I take my medicine and have learned:

1. If I am doing what I am suppose to do I don't worry
2. If I don't worry I don't have extreme emotions
3. If I don't have extreme emotions I have more energy
4. If I have more energy I have a better day
5. If I have a better day then I don't have to worry and I can do what I am suppose to do

Conclusion:

Once I got rewarded from freedom-feelings, shed the trappings of illegal drugs, regained my memories, and don't have hallucinations, the next freedom was to lose the bad habits and thought-cycling. When in time past this firmly established as known fact, I was relieved to remember what I had forgotten. This has led to now----the best year ever since my first taste of hallucinating in 2003.

And what is done I cannot go back and alter. What I can state is that I am horrifically sorry! I am now able to approach a clear understanding of my mental disorganizations. The recovered black-out of what I did has changed me. And being off illegal drugs (meth) has freed me to feel once again, which that pollution was blocking along with my schizophrenia. Books, time, medication, healing and remembering are my miracles.

Editor's note: Mark committed murder in a schizophrenic psychotic state influenced by his use of the illegal drug methamphetamine.

Randy Dean Jones, Sr. #0036042

My name is Randy Dean Jones Sr. # 0036042. I am serving a life sentence for 1st Degree Murder at the Iowa State Penitentiary Ft. Madison, Iowa. I would like to take you on a journey back into my child hood not for you to feel sorry for me or to use as an excuse for my crime only to show you what kind of a person I was and still am and all the hurdles I had to overcome in my life. Let's go back to when I was three years old while on vacation at Spirit Lake I fell in the lake and drowned. My older brother brought me back to life with C.P.R., as a child I had a bad problem wetting the bed, the more I tried to stop the more it happened and the more sever the punishments got. At first my parents would spank me with whatever they could find, one time it would be a belt, another time it would be a fishing pole or even a rose bush limb. When that didn't work, they hung my sheets out the window of my bedroom so all my friends could see them. All my friends made fun of me real bad to the point that I just didn't want to live but somehow I overcame it. My parents told me if I told anyone about the abuse it would get worse. So, then I would run away from home. When I was only 7 or 8 years old that I can remember sometimes my buddy's moms would hide me out till my parents found out and made threats to them. So then I would have to sleep in a field that had tall grass, this was on East 17th or 18th Dean Avenue by the train tracks. I was the youngest out of 8 boys and one girl. My parents got so upset about the bed wetting that they started taking me to all kinds of doctors, these doctors kept telling them I would grow out of it but my parents didn't want to hear it. They kept calling doctors till one said he could stop the bed wetting. I remember going to this doctor's office I want to say it was called Hilltop Clinic in Des Moines, Iowa. Well this doctor put me under and he took an instrument with a razor blade in it, he stuck it all the way in my penis and pulled the razor back out opening the hole of my penis, when I woke up it hurt so bad, this lasted for two weeks. I remember getting so mad at my parents because it didn't work all they did was torture me. I snapped out and ran away from home and slept at the train tracks for a long time before they caught me. That was when I broke into the building at the train tracks to steal some food, and I got caught by the police. My parents sent me to the Boy's home, and I mean a lot of Boys homes until I finely ran away from it when I was 15 years old. This is when my older brother Dale Jones took me in and taught me how to take care of myself. A month after my 16th Birthday on September 8th 1981 I got hit by a car head on while I was riding my motor bike, I went through the windshield of the car and broke out the driver's side window and flew about 125 feet and hit the curb with my head. All I know is that I had died in the street that day and came back to life before they could get me to the Hospital. While I was being worked on the Doctor came out and told my mother that I had passed away. My mother told me that she saw my fingers moving in the clear body bag. She yelled for the doctors and the doctors started working on me again. It took the doctors 13 hours to put me back together. I was sent to a intensive care unit with two broken legs upper and lower with the right leg below the knee had been ripped halfway off but they were able to put it back together. I had knocked my hips out of place, split my head open, and had my nose and part of my face ripped off. I spent the next six months in that critical care unit, until I was put in a regular hospital room. This is where I spent the next year or more. The day that I was able to go home, a blood clot had passed through my lung and into my heart. I was told that they had to shock me to bring me back to life so I had to stay for another week. I had to be put on a Heparin Lock to thin my blood I had to have this for many months. I was sent home in a wheelchair and I was told I would probably never walk again in my life. At one point I had to go to Broadlawns Hospital to get some pins taken out of my leg. When they went to take my pins out of my leg, they didn't clean off the pins first and it gave me a bone infection called Osteomyelitis. I had this infection till 1990. I was still trying to walk at this time. I stopped filling sorry for myself and kept trying to teach myself how to walk again. When I could not walk after two years I just wanted to give up. Not only could I not walk but my face was messed up real bad, people didn't even want to look at me. I tried to commit suicide a couple years after my accident. This old man had to have been my guardian angel, because he sat with me for a very long time and taught me how to better myself and a better way to teach myself how to walk again. I bought a small peddle bike, I asked the doctors if they could put a hinge in the knee of my cast so I would be able to peddle the bike. I went home and for the next 5 years I got on this bike and peddled it all around the East Side of Des Moines, Iowa. After all the many surgeries I had to have. Finely the one day when I stopped, and I put my feet down I could stand up without falling over. I was so happy that day I had forgot all about -my face being messed up because I could stand up on my own. This was the new start that the old man was talking about. I tried to find him but it's like he didn't exist. I had asked everybody around. I even tried looking him up at the library, but I had no luck finding him anywhere. Over the next several years I received plastic surgery on my face. I also had a lot of surgeries having bone grafts done on my right leg. I still had trouble walking but at least I could walk some. One day I met a girl that didn't look away from me. She wanted to date me. So, we dated and fell in love, got married, had three children later on and stayed together for a long time until I found my wife in bed with the minister that had married us. I became a single father with three children. Not long after this a man attacked me in my driveway. As you know now, I could not run at that time. My phone would not dial out. As I was trying to go for help the man jumped on me for the second time down the street, where he pulled a knife on me. I begged this man to stop but he would not. I had gotten away from him once, but I could not run, so he caught me and threw me on the ground. He threatened to kill me, and then go kill my children. He then threatened to go put sexually abuse my two-year-old daughter. At this time, I thought my life was over. I believed that he still had the knife, and I was still fearing for my life, after he said that about my little girl I blacked out. All I remember was coming to and he was lying on the ground next to me. I was so scared I didn't know what to do so I went home. I had just shot a person. All I wanted to do in the first place was to go call the police. I feared for my life and he had given me no other option but to protect myself. What I should have done was call the police anyway, but I was too scared. Shooting this man was the very last thing I wanted to do. If my lawyers had gotten my medical records like I had ask it would have proven my story of this event was true because it would of proved I in fact 100% that I could not run, so I could not have chased this man down. I was convicted of running this man down, over hills, down allies for over three blocks. Don't get me wrong I was in the wrong for having a handgun. I was a single father trying to put a car business together buying and selling cars like my brother Dale Jones at Jones Repair on Murry Street Des Moines Iowa. I had this gun for the protection of myself and my kids. Yes, I should have gotten a permit for it. The only criminal record I had at this time was for driving without a license and a very small weed charge. I had a lot of Des Moines police officers testify that this man made the same threats to them about their kids. In no way is this letter an excuse for my crime in taking a life. I just wanted you to know a little bit about my life and all the trials and tribulations that I have been able to overcome in my life and why I deserve a 2nd chance. Thank you for listening to the story behind this tragedy. My children need their dad.

James Curtis

Hi. My name is James and I want you all to know how my life after 22 years in prison has been.. I want to start off by saying I am proud of the man I've become and hope one day I can become a productive member of society again. So with that being said this is my Life...

I came to prison in 1999 at the age of 19 and was such a knuckle head, still young and on my very first number in prison. I was terrified 160lbs and not a friend in sight. I had to do everything on my own and didn't know anybody, with me being so young and I had to make friends some how and that always led to trouble. I didn't have a care in the world because I knew they couldn't do any worse then they already did so I was catching reports and cell rest and going to the DD unit for report. But this all played on me being young and not knowing how to be a man.

So my first 3 years I didn't accomplish anything but to get in trouble. By now I am 21 and still not very mature because I got questioned for a murder that happened in 1998 and I confessed to it because I thought I was smarter then the law and knew I had a lawyer and anything I said wasn't admissible. But once again my age fooled me again because that was not the case evidently. So in 2001 they arrested me for first degree murder and that when I really got a reality check and got sent to Anamosa state penitentiary. And let me tell you walls are a lot scarier than a fence when you're a 21-year-old kid. But I soon came to find out this was a whole different world and I started hanging out with lifers that have been in for 20 plus years and that's when I started growing up a little bit...I got my GED shortly after I got to Anamosa and got a job in the kitchen as a cook.. Still thought I knew everything and didn't want to follow the rules. Still getting little petty reports for small things nothing serious.

But as years went on I started thinking there has got to be an easier way to do time and that's when I really started to mature and got a job that I could also earn an apprenticeship and that was janitorial service and passed all my tests and got it. You know they say "it's hard to feel a sense of accomplishment in prison" well I'm here to say that lit a fire under me and I wanted more. So, I start applying to the maintenance department, but they always had lifer quotas one of the many

plagues us lifers face while in here. On a certain percentage of us can work in one area at a time... But by god I got my job in maintenance and became a plumber and within a couple years I was lead man of a crew of six inmates and then I became lead man and trouble shooter and I did that for ten years and started my apprenticeship but that was short lived because when the new warden took over he shipped me to Fort Madison. All the stuff they trained me for pipe fitting, pipe threading, troubleshooting, hazmat training. So much about the plumbing field that I know I could run a successful business in the world if that's the road I wanted to go down. But no such luck I got sent to a max prison. 12 years report free and doing the best I had ever done. But I didn't let that bother me because I needed to succeed and show not only myself but the ones that had doubt in me still that I was an adult now. So, when I got here to Fort Madison, I got a good job in IPI and worked there for a while. I then got called on to go work in the kitchen as a cook because I had experience. I did that for a couple years and also while I was here there's no reasons why I couldn't do some groups so I did thinking for change and I also did some A.V.P classes...

But I wanted more so I went back to IPI and worked with my hands again because that's what I like doing. While at IPI I also got my forklift certificate and am now certified and very trained... I would like to go to a medium one day soon but once again with the lifer plague lives are stuck wherever they are for now.

But I just want to say I was still a kid when I committed my crime and would love nothing more than a second chance at life. I have a beautiful girl that loves me and has watched me grow right before her eyes. And family that loves me more than a little bit. I have family that would support me to the end of the world. They have also watched me grow into the man I am today and are so very proud of me.

I am a good example of coming to prison as a child and growing up my record reflects that…

I just want a second chance to prove that...

Thank you...

James Curtis

Omar R. Wilkins-Bey

I, Mr. Omar R. Wilkins-Bey have been incarcerated here, with the Iowa State Penitentiary since 2003.   I will willingly admit that the first 5 years of my life were spent in prison as an ignorant kid, trying to make a place for myself. All that changed with my first encounter with:

Alternative to Violence Project. I have been a proud and learning student of AVP since 2008, working my way to become a facilitator (since 2008). I love this program because it was here that I learned that people actually cared about how I felt, what I thought, how I desired to grow, the problems that were plaguing me, etc. This is where I also learned tools that would assist me with dealing with these problems, external and internal. I will admit that I have been in trouble since my involvement in AVP, but I will honestly say that AVP changed my view of life, people, hope, success and what it means to be a man. This program is run by outside volunteers and that is why it is so successful! Because Men in prison are more inclined to open up and share their trials with people who don't work for the state.

I am also involved with Toastmasters since 2010. I started attending on a whim, I heard they were giving away donuts and coffee, and for a Man in prison those are luxuries that you cannot miss out on! However, the ambience had an air of intellect to it: as well as it was very interactive. I have had the privilege of advancing through Toastmasters. I am an accomplished ACS: Advanced Communicator Silver and a CL; Competent Leader. These are only accomplished by being active member of the group, by participating in leadership roles and just immersing myself in positivity.

I worked at Iowa Prison Industries specifically as a Lean Facilitator. Working a job in prison should be a requirement! This is the only place (besides school) where men are able to learn something of substance! I was privileged enough to work in IPI Woodworking Factory and that is where I earned my Lean Certification.

I am currently involved in the Kitchen/Cook Apprenticeship Program. I have completed my apprenticeship and am still a cook in the prison kitchen. I enjoy studying and taking tests, but more than anything I love challenging to create meals and improvising on the go.

I am also involved in several self-help groups. Project Harmony is one that allows inmates of different backgrounds and races to come together and learn about the different aspects of our respective cultures. I appreciate this program because when you sit and listen to other races or guys from rural areas you come to see that although we come from different places, we all have the same struggles. It is nice to be able to empathize with other human beings. I have been involved since around 2010.

The NAACP has allowed me the opportunity to absorb the plight of people, not just people of color; those who are poor and voiceless as well. The best part of the NAACP is that I have learned how to organize in a positive way, for positive reasons. I have learned how to write proposals as well as just writing period. I have been a member since 2013ish.

I have been the President of both the NAACP and Project Harmony and I have held board position in both of them also.

My hope is that We The People can come to the understanding that prisoners are human beings, just like everyone else. That while incarcerated, prisoners deserve the opportunity to correct their behavior, make amends for their crimes and begin the process of understanding what it takes to be a father, employee, role model and citizen. Without rehabilitation there is little room for hope.

Jerrid Winfrey

Accomplishments since being incarcerated:

- Completed GED program and degree
- SSIP (Suicide/Self Injury, Protocol) Watcher
- Self-rehabilitated surgically repaired knee due to lack of Physical Therapy availability
- Completed Career Readiness Class
- Math Tutor for Prison School
- Testimonial Speaker for "The Domino Effect" for three years
- Testimonial Speaker for a Board of Juvenile Probation Officers
- Completed Treatment class called "Thinking for A Change"
- Enrolled in college courses through Adams State University

To Whom it May Concern

My name is Jerrid Winfrey. I've been incarcerated since I was nineteen. I knew soon after my sentencing that I didn't want to be what the court said I was. I knew I was better than my worst act. I knew I wanted to be a great person. I set out to accomplish that immediately. I started by taking classes while awaiting trial to finish my high school diploma. I was unable to get credits for elective classes and couldn't receive my actual high school diploma. This was very disappointing, but I had to keep going. I was shipped off to prison after spending two years in the county jail. Immediately after arriving to prison I asked to be paced in the GED program here at the Iowa State Penitentiary. I completed my GED after a few months. It was a good feeling but also showed me I could have been so much more. I next went onto be an SSIP (Suicide/Self Injury, Protocol) watcher. I would watch people on suicide watch. It gave me a different perspective on my mental health. It helped me pay attention to it more and address the issues I had with mental health. It was also fulfilling to sit and talk with the guys I was watching and just give them an ear. Try and talk to them about whatever they had going on. Six years after having that job I dislocated my knee and had to have it surgically repaired. I quit my SSIP job and went to work in the gym so I could rehab my knee. . .

Basketball was something I discovered while in prison. It was an escape for me. It gave me a hobby. It gave me something positive to do, while also teaching me about being unselfish. It taught me how to be driven and work hard. I ended up teaching myself the game and became very good at it . . .

I began to notice once arriving at the new I.S.P. in 2015 that I had become very anti-social. I believe it came from the structure of the old prison. It was very segregated. You didn't have much contact with the guards. It gave you a sense of "its' us against them" I always knew that no one was responsible for me being in prison though. I told myself I needed to start opening up more to people, "that I was worthy". I needed to be more social for my own sanity. Slowly but surely I started to. In the process I started to become the person I knew I was. I took career readiness classes and received a certificate for that. It showed me that as long as I applied myself I would be good at almost any job.

For seven years I was report free while being incarcerated, that all changed on July 17, 2017. On July 1st there was a race riot on the yard. I knew it was brewing beforehand and was able to tell myself to stay out of it, it wasn't my fight to fight. I had a different mission. I was able to avoid getting into the riot by the prison was place on lockdown. I couldn't understand how everyone was being punished for what some people did. I used my stress as an excuse to get high. I smoked a joint with my cellmate at the time. The next day I was given a UA test and it tested positive for marijuana. I was sent to the hole and given thirty days there. I knew I shouldn't have done it in the first place. I decided I was going to admit my guilt and take responsibility for my actions. This may have been the first time I ever thought like this. I decided to just take my time and not appeal the thirty days of hole time decision.

I next went on to be a math tutor here at the prison's school. I helped a lot of guys pass their math Hi-Set test. It was amazing being able to help someone work towards their goals. It gave me my first real sense of purpose. It showed me that I am a great person. That I can learn anything, and that it's in my nature to want to help people. Espccially guys that come from the environment I come from. I quickly noticed that most of the students were African American. It was the first time I felt like I was helping my community versus hurting it, the feeling was short lived. After having the tutor job for eighteen months I convinced myself that it would be ok for me to look at porn on my work computer. I ultimately was sent to the hole for it. This gave me my second disciplinary report of my incarceration. I was forced to re-evaluate myself. I took full advantage of it. I once again decided I would admit my guilt and just take my time without appealing. I was given thirty days in the hole. Those thirty days were the hardest days of my stay here. It was if the entire amount of time that I've been incarcerated hit me all at once. It really made me take a look in the mirror. I told myself that I was better than this, that I have to be better, and that it's unacceptable for me to still be making these kinds of mistakes . . .

I've taken and completed a computer apprenticeship. I've spoken at an event called "The Domino Effect", three times. Helping educators by sharing my experiences with school I've spoken to a board of juvenile probations officers looking for ideas to better serve the youth. I'm currently enrolled in a college course through Adams State University. I just took my first exam. I just recently finished taking a treatment class called "Thinking For A Change". I've attempted to accomplish all that I can. There isn't much available here at the Iowa State Penitentiary. I've been forced to rehabilitate myself. Out of the things I have accomplished, I am most proud of using my influence in a positive way. I have worked on myself the entire time I have been locked up. I am most proud of trying to help other guys who do have outdates try to see that the life we were living made no sense. To help them see that they do have the potential to be something else in life. To me that is the biggest accomplishment of my time here. . .

At 19 I was given a life sentence. I was told that there was no hope for me. I was a lost cause. I decided not to listen to that. I knew I was more and believed in myself. It's been a long journey and it's not over yet, but I know I'm headed in the right direction. I changed my thinking and was able to grow as a person, and as a man. I did this with no hope of redemption, no hope of freedom. I can only imagine the accomplishments I can achieve if I were given hope, given a chance at redemption . . .

How has prison changed you for the better? How has it changed you for the worse?

Prison has definitely changed me. For the most part it's changed me for the better. I really can't think of too many ways it's changed me for the negative. I'll have to think more on it... Prison has turned me into a man. Prison forced me to slow down. It forced me to realize the things I find important. Like family. Like being ambitious and driven. Like being a leader. It forced me to see these things but find positive ways to achieve these things. Prison really taught me to think. I've always been intelligent, but I never stopped and just thought about everything that was going on around me. Being too smart for my own good was always a problem for me. Prison showed me that I like to figure things out on my own. It showed me that being self- sufficient was important to me. I try to teach myself how to do any and everything I might need to know in life. Little things like knowing how to cut my own hair. Big things like knowing the law. Things of that nature. Prison forced me to grow up. I've technically grew up here. It's scary to think about but it's the reality of my situation...

What's different about you now?

The number one thing that's different about me now is me thinking. Me responding versus reacting. I was selfish when I was out. I didn't have much of a conscious. Now I'm so understanding. So forgiving. Those were two things I was lacking out there. I was understanding and forgiving for the people I feel like I loved, but I wasn't for everyone else... Another thing is I know how to control my emotions now. I know how to not only see them but address the root emotion. Knowing the difference between hurt and anger helped me tremendously. Understanding that the world is not against me. Understanding that things will not always go my way and this ok because those types of things make us who we are... I'm so even keeled now. I just feel like I get life now. Nothing takes me too high. Nothing takes me too low. Prison has made me such a patient person; it's humbled me unbelievably. It makes me laugh when I think about it... It's showed me that life is entirely too short. That our focus should be on love and happiness and not all of the things we get distracted by out there...

When I really think about it though I haven't changed. I've grown. I'm still a passionate person. I'm still a protector by nature. I'm still a loyal person. I've learned to be those same things but in a positive way. That's where my growth has made me such a better person. A better man. I thought I knew it all at fifteen. I thought I had the world figured out. When I look back at it all I just wish I could have been strong enough to overcome my environment. Over the years I've seen so many people who've made it out of similar circumstances and I just applaud them for it because I know how hard it is to do...

How is your mental health?

My mental health is very well considering my situation. Considering I've been locked up since 19. Given no hope. People around me giving up on me. Society essentially saying I'm a lost cause... Somehow through it all I've seen the light. I realized I had nothing to complain about. I know why I'm here. The only thing I can do is be better. I told myself that is what I'd do. I told myself that it can always be worse. That there are plenty of people who are worse off than me. That mindset led me to strive for more. It allowed me to be happy in a place where you'd think you wouldn't see happiness, where you'd think you couldn't achieve happiness. My mental health is good... The one occasion it wasn't was about a year and a half ago. I went to the hole and it just was too much for me at the time. It's like the walls were caving in on me. I dealt with depression for the first time. It's as if a different reality set in on me. For the first time ever I felt helpless. I felt hopeless. It was the first time where I felt alone. Even with people in my corner. I knew they couldn't relate to what I was going through so their presence did nothing for me. It was all in my mind though. Both my mother and father were there for me. They really helped me out of it. I had a pen pal in Canada at the time and she really helped me out of it. It lasted a few months... I noticed it immediately. Seeing it and acknowledging it was the best thing I could have done. It allowed me to address it head on. Luckily, I was able to get through it and come out stronger. Ever since I've been in such a higher place mentally. I had to realize that I've been blessed my entire life and just didn't know it. I thought about all of the blessings I've had growing up and just missed out on. I thought about all the blessings I've had since being in prison and I told myself it was time to make that final step as a man and reach my full potential...

Do you have friends in there? Are they nice to you in there?

I have a lot of "friends", in general in here. As far as what I would classify as a friend though I only have one. I believe a friend cares about your well-being. A friend only wants to see you do good. A friend only wants to help you do good. I believe friends are people who love you and want nothing in return for their friendship. So with that definition I only have one in here. That's good though. I have a lot of associates. I've become a very social person. It wasn't like that my first five years. It was something I had to fix for myself. I noticed that me being antisocial wasn't good for my mental health and went on to be better about opening up with guards and inmates. It was one of the best things I could have done for my growth as a person. Now I'm an open book. Even with complete strangers. I'm not afraid to share anything. I'm not afraid to cry in front of grown men who I know will judge me in here. I'm just comfortable with who I am as a man and know I have nothing to be ashamed about...
Prison isn't like the movies. People are very respectful here for the most part. Even the guards aren't as bad as you would assume...

Nicholas Hanegan

My name is Nicholas Hanegan and I am serving a life sentence for first degree kidnapping and attempted murder-a crime I committed shortly after my twenty-third birthday. This happened nearly two decades ago. If there is one thing I would change it wouldn't be my situation, but how the judicial system rehabilitates incarcerated individuals. This is my struggle, and I wish to tell you my story in hopes someone close to you, or in a similar situation doesn't end up like me.

The self-image of who I am was destroyed when I committed my crime. After the initial reality of what my actions caused to another human-being surfaced through the haze of methamphetamine psychosis, I immediately panicked and sought to end my life. With the aid of the Department of Corrections and the people working to serve it, I have been given the opportunity to face my inner turmoil head-on. This in turn has allowed me to find humanity and a small piece of redemption through the opportunities offered to those incarcerated.

My story begins at the age of twenty-one when I was first introduced to methamphetamine for the first time in the state capitol of Des Moines, Iowa. With my struggles with depression and ADHD, I found I couldn't cope with the world around me, and I couldn't afford insurance to get the treatment I so desperately needed. This in turn led to self-medicating, but with a poisonous substance that literally consumed my entire being.

Within two years I found myself in full blown meth-psychosis, losing touch with the world around me as if I were in a nightmare I couldn't control. It is hard to describe the experience to someone who has never had one, but the best way to put it is like your brain is misfiring, and the thoughts coming through are no longer your own, distorted and fragmented, like pieces of a puzzle you can never put together.

In the peak of my psychosis, I tried to kill a young woman in 2000, by the grace of God, I wasn't successful. I take full accountability for my actions. But how can I change what has happened? How can a full life spent in a prison correct my wrongs to the person I hurt and pay my debt back to society? These and many other questions flood my brain as I walk the halls at IMCC, wondering what I can do in the here in now to make sure something like this never happens again, yet still remain human, as I wait to slowly age then die in this institution?

I wake up in the morning and the first thing that comes to my mind is "I hope the person I harmed is safe."

Then the questions follow. "Is this person happy? What if I never came into their life, what can I do today to atone for what I have done? I go to church and pray. I volunteer on the special need's unit as a mentor for those who are suffering from diminished capacity, yet something isn't clicking. Something is terribly wrong with my life.

Empathy is the sole reason I exist. I feel the pain I have caused; I search for the words but they don't surface. Just emotions. Like colors on a spectrum only I can see. Guilt, shame, remorse. Pity. Pity for myself, which turns to a self-deserving mind-set, like I deserve this punishment and I need to die, old and alone in this place.

Someday I am struck deeply for what I have done. But others, I am suffocated.

These, and many other factors have led me to what is termed the word-REDEMPTION.

Can I be redeemed? Do I have to spend the rest of my life in prison for my transgressions, or is there a way to pay the debt I owe to society in a more sustainable way?

Prison is full of opportunities to change. Some of the incarcerated individuals who walk through the fated iron fence take full advantage of these opportunities, and others do not. It doesn't necessarily make them bad people for not bettering themselves, it simply means they are not ready.

I have spent the last twenty years of my life doing everything I can to be a better person, for myself, and to the world I have offended with my crimes. In 2011, I completed an A.A. in Liberal Arts from Adams State University. In 2012, I was awarded the Colorado Extended Studies Scholarship, which helped me continue furthering my success. In 2013, I completed an apprenticeship through the

U.S. Department of Labor to be a computer peripheral equipment operator, that same year I was granted a certificate at the customer service academy through Pueblo Community College. The classes taught me a variety of special topics on human relations, such as working with those with disabilities and the elderly. In 2018, I finished the entrepreneurship courses taught by Adams State, and also earned a certificate for 45 contact hours in Alternative Dispute Resolution. This taught me to resolve conflict without violence, and how to de-escalate a situation with logic and a calm demeanor. With all of these accomplishments behind me, I have also been a mentor for the special need's population here at IMCC, and I am currently pursuing a bachelor's degree in Liberal Arts from the University of Iowa.

But I have to ask, why?

Why am I given all these opportunities to better myself if I am never going to be released from prison? How is this sustainable to the general public?

The truth is, it's not.

When the State of Iowa granted me life in prison without the possibility of parole the message was very clear. YOU ARE NOT CAPABLE OF REDEMPTION.

I have spent the last twenty years trying my best to correct my wrongs. Why can I not be redeemed? Why can I not have a second chance at freedom?

I know for a fact that the skills I have developed since my incarceration can help society in better ways. I can mentor those with special needs and volunteer to aid the elderly. With my degrees I can get a job as a counselor, using my story as a premise to help troubled children. I can further my education at the University and bring new ideas to the criminal justice system to make it more effective in areas that have gone overlooked. My heart and mind are in the right place. Yet...something is wrong.

I am going to die without ever being able to use the skills the State of Iowa spend valuable resources on. This is the most wasteful sense of depravity I could have ever imagined. If I am not capable of redemption then why waste resources on trying to make me a better if you are going to hold me in an institution until death?

I ask for a second chance at life. Give me the opportunity to pay my debt back to society. So much has been spent on my rehabilitation, utilize what you have created! Me-the mentor, entrepreneur, scholar, activist, and human-being. I am capable of so much more beyond these walls. I wrote this article to bring attention to the concept of redemption. This is a call to action. Everyone is capable of redemption. If they were not, then the State would simply execute those convicted of life instead of making them better. We are one step away at resolving a whole new issue. Giving those with life in prison a second chance at parole. Please take the factors I have written into consideration and apply them in a practical sense. We as a society can do better. We as a people are capable of redemption.

Frederick Babino-Bey

My name is Frederick Babino-Bey. I am a 47-year-old Black American. I was born in San Francisco, California and raised in Columbia, Louisiana. I have been serving Life in the state of Iowa since 2001.

When I first came to prison, I spent a lot of time asking myself how I got here. I was unable to answer that question for a long time. I knew the specifics of how I got here. I took another human beings' life; but I did not believe myself to be a killer. I man a cold-blooded heartless person with no respect for human life. Over thee years, time forced me to look back at the life that I had lived and the choices that I made in my past.

As I tried to adjust to a life behind bars, I began to take a long, hard look at the person I had become and the person that I wanted to be. I knew that I had to make changes, however I did not know where to begin. The first thing that I decided to do was to get a job, learn a skill and the responsibility of work. I also figured that this would keep me out of trouble. So I got a job in the furniture shop here in prison. Through this job and the staff members that I have worked for over the years, I have had the opportunity to learn many new skills. At the same time, I was learning to be accountable and responsible, while I did not realize the impact that this was having on me personally. I did begin to realize that I was beginning to think differently. I was beginning to make choices that were in my best interest and not hat I thought made me look or feel good. This new attitude led me to start looking at what I held important and I realized that I needed to make the best out of this situation. So I started to read books to educate myself. However, after years of reading books and gaining some knowledge, I was still not making the best decisions, even when it was my intention to make the right decision. This led me to start to question why I was making these wrong decisions, and I realized that it was because I didn't know how to think. I thought back on my time before prison, and I realized that even back then I wasn't making bad decisions because I was a bad person; I was making these choices because I was not thinking. After this profound realization, I started out on a journey to learn to be a thinker. I started attending self-help groups, like Alternatives to Violence, NAACP, Project Harmony, Humanist Group and Toastmasters. I also signed up for treatment programs like Thinking for a Change, a critical thinking program. All of these groups helped me in my journey to learn how to think, but ultimately, it was my own desire to change my thinking that made the biggest difference. After the tools gained from these groups, I did some deep soul searching, and I realized that I had always been looking for the easy way out, the easy answer. Somewhere along the way I learned that when faced with the right and wrong choice, always choose the right one, and everything else would fall into place. This seemed to simplistic, but I decided to give it a try, and soon found that things were changing for the better for me. And, ironically, things are becoming easier for me. In the end, I learned that I needed to embark on a journey of self-mastery, and so today I am working on mastering my thoughts, my Self. I am facing down on obstacle (foe) at a time and trying to live up to my highest potential.

My accomplishments thus far have been:

- I have worked at the same job for 10 years
- I have attained a cabinet making certification
- I have earned a Lean Principle's Certification
- I have a Forklift Certification
- I recently completed a Pumps and Valves Certification
- I have been a Hospice volunteer since 2009

There have been a lot of people here at the prison that have been a huge help to me, numerous staff members, as well as many fellow prisoners. I am also a student of spiritual teachings. While I don't align myself to any particular religion, I stud and participate in the moral conduct, right belief of all spiritual teachings. I am a work in progress, but I now recognize and acknowledge my responsibility to humanity, and I am striving to be the best person I can be.

Sean O'Geary

Some believe no one with LWOP deserves a second chance. Until (God forbid) something happens with one of their loved ones. Then the thought process changes. They know if given a second chance that person wouldn't engage in the high-risk factors that got them in that position. They can identify because of the closeness they share. Should that person be demonized and held in stasis for a mistake they made decades ago?

I was 21 when sentenced to LWOP. As I sat in the cell, I began reflecting on conversations I had with my family. It's one thing you have an abundance of; time to think. I took an inventory on what I wanted to change and accomplish. It was overwhelming and the predicament I found myself in made it even worse.

They say you only live once. So I had to make a choice. Continue down the road that got me here or change. In order to have positive changes we need to make positive choices. Sounds simple right? All around me is negativity and excuses. Excuses people made for their actions. Negativity in those who would not try because of their own self-defeating and selfish attitudes. I could have chosen to immerse myself in this ocean of despair. Easily. To start I've spent the last 22 years convicted of a crime I did not commit. But once you're convicted you can't just say it. You have to prove it. Giving up would have been so easy. I think that's why most do.

I started my journey earning a 2-year degree. I tried to when I was free but drugs and having fun seemed more important. I went on obtaining credits from University of Iowa and Ohio University. I took all the programs my counselor requested.

My Mom always said, "The mind and body go hand in hand". It's true. As I improved my mind so too did my body. I gained so much weight because of depression. I lost 65 pounds and got myself back to the form I had when I wrestled in high school. You may think it's easy to work out because of the time we have. It's not. It's a choice. Most that do use it to pass the time, not for goals to achieve.

Since I lost weight I was able to play sports again. I took up soccer, softball, and basketball. In all I set personal goals. Learning so much from my teammates. Now I try to pass on what I've learned to others. Practice makes perfect my Mother always said.

As time passed I began looking for other ways to improve. It's hard for a lifer to take part in programs because those who are returning to Society have priority. In most instances' lifers cannot even apply. So, I began teaching myself Spanish. This has been an ongoing process and to this day I am not fluent. I can speak better than understand. It is more of a hobby now.

Throughout the years a guy we called Tater Head would ask me to try my hand at wood working. I declined because I literally knew nothing about it. I eventually made the choice to try. To see what it was about. I found everyone there was willing to pass on their expertise in the areas they knew. I began saying this place was the best kept secret this side of the Mississippi. These guys were great. Over the years I learned the best techniques from each one. I read about other ways too. Some are great at building, some at finishing, and some at intarsia and inlay. I wanted to be good at everything. With their help I turned myself into a great wood worker. And I literally knew nothing about it. The projects I made I am able to give away as gifts or my family sells.

One day I was watching one of the St. Jude commercials. The one where the kids have cancer. I've always hated the disease. I was young when my grandmother died from it. What it did to her stuck with me all these years. Watching the TV I began to tear up thinking how unfair life can be and what these kids had to go through. I could identify with them in that they stayed positive even through the worst of times. I called my Mom and told her I wanted to take the money I made through wood working and donate to them. My Mom and I have been doing this for 10 years now. Those kids will write sometimes, and Mom will send them to me. I'm just happy I can do something for someone else. They deserve it.

As I matured, I joined a prison sanctioned group called CHANGE. Within a few months I was elected to treasurer. I liked that we had to pay a membership fee to join. Because of it we all knew we were there to make our community better. We either sponsored or created programs. Donating our time for chess tournaments, CrossFit competitions and run/walk-a-thons. The money raised would go to heart and breast cancer research. We created a program where dads could record reading a short story to their kids and send the video to them. Through other fundraisers we donated thousands of dollars to Camp Courageous, Boys and Girls clubs, and disaster relief funds across the country. Sadly, this group was shut down by the administration. They said it was because of a lack of staffing.

My experiences in CHANGE group caused me to run for a seat on the Council. It is a governing body within the prison. We work with the administration to address issues that affect the community. In addition, we help the incarcerated to effectively deal with the everyday problems we all go through. It is like CHANGE group only I found out real quick not everyone has the same agendas.

At the end of last year (2019) the administration wanted to remake Council into something smaller and more efficient. I took it upon myself to work with the treatment director and rewrite the by-laws. We are voted in by those in our living units. And our terms are for one year. In our living unit only four are voted in. Over twenty ran and I was one of the four.

Through the COVID pandemic we came up with ideas to keep the population safe. We tried to put forth the administration's ideas as to always wearing a mask. I took my personal time to wipe down things within the cell house with bleach. For 8-9 months we didn't have a single case. Sadly though it got in and we are going through a lock down now I've never seen here at the prison. This has put a cog into some of the things I still wanted to accomplish this year. I hope to be elected to another term and establish groups like AVP (Alternative to Violence Program) and Toastmasters.

Bad things happen to good people. It's the choices we make as to what we want to do with what we are now and who we want to be. It is a choice we make to better ourselves and others. To rise up out of the squalor that is our lives. Like the mythical Phoenix that rises from the ashes of death every day to be reborn.

You may be thinking, "but how do we choose the ones who have changed from those who haven't?" Or as I say from the "pretenders". The answer is in their ACTIONS. My Mom always said, "ACTIONS speak louder than WORDS".

It's true in here as it is out there. People make a CHOICE to change. This change is shown through their actions. It does not happen overnight but is a constant process we carry throughout our lives. It becomes clear as day when one is asked, "how have you changed?" You will see a constant progression as they answer. But the answer is in the ACTIONS they have taken; not just the WORDS they speak.

I want to leave you with this. I said earlier we only live once. But this isn't true. We only die once but we live every day.

My Conclusion

by Sue Hutchins

I have learned so much about the incarcerated and their loved ones over the years. I have also learned the difference between punishment, rehabilitation, revenge and our need for reconciliation as a society. And now I have had the opportunity to introduce you to some of the people who are doing a life sentence without the possibility of parole in Iowa's prison system.

I so hope this book, their book, has given you an insight into the way people choose to change as they mature, gain empathy, and make better decisions.

Any and all proceeds from the sale of this book will be donated to non-profit agencies that assist inmates and their loved ones. There is no financial gain for the contributors.

I am closing this collection of writings by these 27 Lifers in Iowa prisons with a poem written by **Travis Wolfkill**

Questions From Inside

I live in a human zoo

An evolved animal

Like you I have feelings

And I can think rational

When does the punishment end?

When does the rehabilitation begin?

How can we be restored to our former state

If we were criminals at the gate?

What is the fate of a boy

Who became a man

Who became a conscious communicator

Instead of a hater?

Again, I ask----

When does the punishment end?

Death Row and all the souls

Who died in the Pen

Was it necessary

Or

Should we try and forgive?

CONTRIBUTORS (in no particular order)

Gary Titus

Michael Blackwell

Steve Tryon

Stanley L. Hart III

Travon Jones, Uriyel

Eid Nassif

Cedric B. Theus

Carlos Robinson-El

John Epps

Anonymous

Ramale Hunt

Christine Shepard

David Foell

Imere Hall

Jason Hiveley

Travis Wolfkill

Jeffrey Hoover

Keith Bruns

Kline Goeders

Mark Becker

Randy Jones

James Curtis

Omar Wilkins-Bey

Jerrid Winfrey

Nicholas Hanegan

Frederick Babino-Bey

Sean O'Geary

IOWA Prisons

ISP   -   Iowa State Penitentiary, Ft. Madison

ASP   -   Anamosa State Penitentiary, Anamosa

FDCF - Ft. Dodge Correctional Facility, Ft. Dodge

MPCC – Mt. Pleasant Correctional Facility, Mt. Pleasant

NCCF – North Central Correctional Facility, Rockwell City

ICIW   -   Iowa Correctional Institution for Women, Mitchellville

NCF   -   Newton Correctional Facility, Newton

IMCC - Iowa Medical Classification Center, Coralville

CCF   -   Clarinda Correctional Facility, Clarinda

Prepared by:

Sue Hutchins

PO Box 835

Marion, Iowa 52302

575 343-0202

hutchins_sue@yahoo.com